CW01262401

Victorian Recipes with a Side of Scandal

THE STORY OF ETHEL BARRY

SHERRY MONAHAN

OTTERFORD
BENTONVILLE, ARKANSAS

OTTERFORD

An Imprint of Roan & Weatherford Publishing Associates, LLC
Bentonville, Arkansas
www.roanweatherford.com

Copyright © 2024 by Sherry Monahan

We are a strong supporter of copyright. Copyright represents creativity, diversity, and free speech, and provides the very foundation from which culture is built. We appreciate you buying the authorized edition of this book and for complying with applicable copyright laws by not reproducing, scanning, or distributing any part of it in any form without permission. Thank you for supporting our writers and allowing us to continue publishing their books.

Library of Congress Cataloging-in-Publication Data
Names: Monahan, Sherry, author.
Title: Victorian Recipes With a Side of Scandal
Description: First Edition | Bentonville: Otterford, 2024.
Identifiers: LCCN: 2024946558 | ISBN: 978-1-63373-921-5 (hardcover) |
ISBN: 978-1-63373-922-2 (trade paperback) | ISBN: 978-1-63373-923-9 (eBook)
Subjects: | BISAC: COOKING/Courses & Dishes/General |
COOKING/Essays & Narratives | COOKING/Regional & Cultural/English, Scottish & Welsh
LC record available at: https://lccn.loc.gov/2024946558

Otterford Gourmet hardcover edition April, 2025

Cover Design by Casey W. Cowan
Interior Design by Casey W. Cowan, Michele Jones & George "Clay" Mitchell
Editing by Amy Cowan & Michelle Mitchell

This cookbook is a work of historical narrative and culinary exploration. While every effort has been made to accurately portray historical events, customs, and recipes, the author has occasionally drawn on creative interpretation and anecdotal sources to provide context and enrich the storytelling. Some details, including names and locations, may have been modified or adapted for narrative clarity. The recipes included are inspired by historical practices but have been adjusted in some cases to suit modern kitchens and tastes. Readers should exercise caution when preparing recipes, especially those involving unfamiliar techniques or ingredients, and adapt them as necessary to meet dietary or safety considerations. This work is not intended to defame or misrepresent any individual, group, or entity. Any resemblance to actual persons, living or deceased, is purely coincidental.

*To my husband, my mother, and friends and colleagues
who have listened to me talk about Ethel since 2009—thank you!*

TABLE OF CONTENTS

INGREDIENT GUIDE	v
INTRODUCTION	vi
ETHEL'S BEGINNINGS	5
BREAKFAST, TEA TIME & BEVERAGES	9
SOUPS, SALADS & CONDIMENTS	37
VEGETABLE & SIDE DISHES	45
MAIN MEALS	61
DESSERTS	81
THE END OF ETHEL	101
INDEX	111
RECIPE CREDITS	115
ACKNOWLEDGMENTS	121
ABOUT THE AUTHOR	122

INGREDIENT GUIDE

For clarity in recipes, this code of ingredients will help ensure the dishes will turn out as intended. For recipes that call for Mason or canning jars, please sterilize the jars and lids according to the manufacturer's directions.

Ingredient Listed	Meaning
Flour	All-Purpose
Butter	Salted Butter
Milk	Whole Milk
Sugar	White, Granulated
Peppers	Green Bell
Onions	White
Eggs	Large
Spices	Ground

INTRODUCTION

Victorian Recipes with a Side of Scandal isn't a typical cookbook, but then again, neither was the life of Ethel Barry. These recipes and stories take you on a Victorian culinary journey like no other. It includes yummy recipes that are spiced up with tantalizing tales of her life.

Before we tuck in, though, I'd like to introduce you to Ethel Marion Barry. She was an English socialite who often made scandalous and shocking decisions during her seventy-four years. By all accounts, she had the makings of becoming a proper Victorian lady. She attended good schools, her grandfathers were vicars, she came from money, and lived in well-to-do London suburbs during the 1800s. Despite that, neither she, nor her parents, held titles like Lord or Lady.

According to Victorian standards, she would marry a nobleman of wealth in her own class, set up house, hold teas, and manage a household staff. But it was her independent, strong-willed attitude that caused Ethel to selectively follow proper protocols in making her life choices. She adhered to them when it came to attire, dining, and manners, but when it came to her wants and desires, she tossed etiquette aside like last year's fashions.

Social standing and etiquette were critical during Queen Victoria's reign, which lasted for more than half of the nineteenth century. Women were considered scandalous for something as small as showing her ankles with too-short of a dress or going "downstairs" to mingle with the kitchen staff. It was a time when girls were brought up to be devoted wives who looked after her house and family or did charity work if she remained single. Young women were schooled on many things, including the importance of getting the right man in her social circle, but not household chores. Men and women married in their own classes, and it was often scandalous when one married above or below their "station."

Follow Ethel's journey through her acquired love of food and cooking. She never dreamed she'd be forced to do domestic chores like laundry and cooking, but her decisions made that a reality. Because her husband took her to America with no staff, she was instructed by her mother's kitchen staff on the basics of roasting meat and baking bread. She donned an apron and measured flour, kneaded bread, cut and seasoned meat, and learned to use a hot oven. However, cooking turned out to be her salvation as she moved from coast to coast. Her story is told from firsthand accounts, old newspapers, and family stories. The recipes are dishes she either recalled, enjoyed on her journey through life, or created, which was one of her proud accomplishments in life.

Sherry

ETHEL'S BEGINNING

HER STORY

Ethel Marion Barry came into the world on April 20, 1864, in Putney, Wandsworth, Middlesex County. When she was about three, her family moved to a London suburb called Lewisham where she spent most of her childhood at their home, called Chesterfield Lodge. Back in the day, the English named their houses, and the name was used to refer to their address. By 1870, her father bought 80 Lawrie Park, aka Gloucester Lodge, in the stately district of Sydenham Hill. The 1859 home sat on a tree-canopied street and was a three-story brick building with beautiful gardens and an enclosed brick wall. Her family's staff included a nurse, housemaid, and a cook.

Ethel was the only daughter of noted composer and musician Charles Ainslie Barry and grew up with five brothers. He composed hymns, cantatas, and other works and was the author of the Analytic Notes to the Crystal Palace, Philharmonic, Richter, and Birmingham concerts. He was the son of Reverend Charles Upham Barry of Ryde, Isle of Wight. Her mother was Edith Bird and the daughter of the Reverend Roger Bird. Ethel and her mother were also grandnieces to England's most well-known nineteenth century painter, Thomas Lawrence. He painted portraits of noted English society members, including a Portrait of George IV and the famous "Pinkie."

After attending all the right schools and being engaged, everything seemed to be falling into place for Ethel, until she met Gerald Hertslet at a London theater. Ethel was said to be playing Juliet in the play, Romeo and Juliet, and he became enamored with her. She returned his affection and neither cared that she was an actress and betrothed to another. She jilted her intended for Gerald, who was above her station, for passion and infatuation. Gerald's father called the marriage a mésalliance, which means a marriage with someone who is considered socially inferior—in this case, the daughter of an eminent London musician. Gerald's father and mother carried the titles of Lord and Lady, and he worked for the King. Theirs was a wedding that neither bride nor groom's parents wanted.

Their relationship moved quickly, and on the morning of April 8, 1885, Ethel stepped into an elegant wedding dress of white silk and lace as she prepared to wed Gerald. Her hair was pinned up, and her veil, trimmed with perfumed orange blossoms and gardenias, was placed on her head. Her maid of honor, Rose Nanette Fenwick, wore a white muslin dress that was trimmed with yellow lace and a matching white hat adorned with yellow feathers. The women arrived at St. Mary Magdalene's Church in Richmond, Surrey. Gerald stood waiting at the altar where he had been baptized back in 1859, shortly after his birth on January 6. The church was filled with hanging baskets and colorful arrangements since Easter had just been celebrated the previous Sunday. Rose led the way down the aisle carrying a basket of yellow daffodils and was followed by Ethel who carried a bouquet of white lilacs as she walked toward her future husband. Gerald, along with his brother and best man Louis, watched as Ethel made her way down the aisle. The two were an attractive couple at the altar. She was a willowy 5'6" blonde, with hazel eyes, and he was striking, with dark hair and a thick Victorian moustache. They exchanged their vows and were pronounced husband and wife.

Many of their relatives and friends, including Gerald's parents, Sir Edward and Lady Hertslet, Ethel's mother, Mrs. Edith Barry, Ethel's brother, Lieutenant Felix Barry, and his wife, Emmeline, and mutual chum, Henry Brandram, looked on. After the ceremony, the wedding guests were invited back to the sprawling Hertslet estate called Belle Vue House. It was built in 1414 on the River Thames and is where Gerald was born and raised. He and his eight siblings, along with a host of servants, occupied the six-story manor. A formal post-wedding breakfast was served in the dining room as guests overlooked the Thames. Ethel's father Charles was notably absent from the wedding and the breakfast. While multiple toasts to a couples' good health and fortune were common at the time, that was not the case for Ethel and Gerald. Only one simple toast was made by St. Mary Magdalene's parish vicar, who said, "The health of the bride and bridegroom." Early that afternoon, Ethel and Gerald left for a brief honeymoon in London before they departed for America.

Facing financial ruin, Gerald, Louis, and a third brother named Bernard, decided to try their luck in an American endeavor so Gerald and his brother Louis could regain their lost fortune from bad investments. They chose California and had some inkling about what they would do once they arrived, but nothing was certain. They contemplated either mining or ranching, despite having no knowledge in either. No matter, they'd figure it out when they got there.

Ethel was so taken with Gerald that she married him fully knowing he had no solid prospects, other than a thousand pounds from Sir Edward. His brothers were given the same. Ethel was also given a yearly allowance of five hundred pounds from her parents. Even though she was happy and infatuated with Gerald, she was not excited about leaving England. She was leaving her family and friends and a comfortable life and being forced to learn the menial tasks that her servants handled. Having no domestic skills proved problematic as she was embarking on her new journey. Ethel had no clue how to survive on her own, let alone take care of a husband. As a young spouse of an English Lord's son, she would have had a staff of her own to manage and not have to do the work herself.

With her fate set in motion, the newlyweds set sail for America with the hope of becoming rich. Their trunks were packed with many necessities, including their new wedding gifts, to start a fine Victorian home. Ethel packed linens, silver, china, saddles, aprons, lace, and more. She would order other kitchen and dining items once they settled into their new home across the pond. Gerald took a few practical items but also took mementos of his English social life, including his sailing and rowing trophies. Once packed, they set out northwest to Liverpool to embark on their American journey.

BREAKFAST, TEA TIME & BEVERAGES

PORRIDGE 9

ICE CREAM SODA 11

STRAWBERRIES & WHIPPED CREAM 12

WHITE BREAD 14

ROCK CAKES 17

CURRANT LOAF 18

SOURDOUGH BREAD 20

SCRAMBLED EGGS 21

CURRIED EGGS 22

APPLE JELLY 23

PORT WINE JELLY 24

APRICOT JAM 26

PEACH JAM 27

MARMALADE TARTLETS 29

CHEESECAKE TARTS 29

APPLE JELLY TARTS 30

APPLE TART 31

PEACH TART 32

BLACKBERRY TART 32

TEA 34

RUSSIAN COCKTAIL 35

GIN FIZZ 36

8 · VICTORIAN RECIPES WITH A SIDE OF SCANDAL

Porridge

Ethel, Gerald, Louis, and Bernard Hertslet and Henry Brandram arrived in Liverpool on Thursday, April 16, 1885, to board the S.S. *Britannic* for their journey to America. Once onboard, Ethel settled into her stateroom and home for the next ten days. Despite her sorrow of leaving England and her family, she was anxiously excited to begin her new life in America. While onboard, she penned, *"I wish we could have begun our new life at once. This inactivity, with nothing to do but think, makes us dreadfully home-sick."* Every morning, after she and Gerald awoke in their stateroom, a member of the *Britannic's* staff served them tea in their room. After tea, they washed up in a basin and dressed for the day. After being seasick for a few days, she adjusted to life on the ocean, and her journey became tolerable. She started taking breakfast in the grand dining room where some of her choices included Finnon Haddies, fried fresh fish, broiled ham and eggs, porridge, and Irish stew. She also ventured out on the deck for fresh air despite the cold temperatures of about thirty-seven degrees and biting wind. Ethel also made porridge or "mush," as it was called it in Lake County, for breakfast.

Serves 1

1/2 cup oatmeal Water, enough to cover oatmeal 1 1/2 cups water Pinch of salt	1. Place the oatmeal in a glass bowl and add just enough water to cover it. Let sit overnight. You can skip this step if you like, but it makes the oatmeal very creamy and soft. 2. In the morning, place the oatmeal in a saucepan and add the water (you can also use milk to make it extra creamy, and then it's called milk porridge). 3. Bring to a boil, reduce the heat to simmer for 4-5 minutes, stirring occasionally so it doesn't stick. Once the oatmeal has softened and thickened, remove from the heat and add the salt. 4. To serve, pour into bowl and top with some milk, cream, honey, or brown sugar. Top with fresh or dried fruits if you like.

ETHEL & THE BOYS SET SAIL

The newlyweds embarked on their journey with two of Gerald's brothers, Louis and Bernard, as well as their mutual friend, Henry Brandram. Henry was the son of Samuel Brandram, an English barrister who also lived in Richmond, Surrey. Even though Henry's father was a barrister by trade, his true love was the theater, and he had a gift and a passion for the oration of Shakespeare plays. Henry was the perfect friend and also the possible connection between Gerald and Ethel. The Hertslet brothers were highly educated and never knew a day of manual labor in their white-collar life. Gerald attended King's College School in London where he intended to study law but only stayed for the spring term in 1875. After leaving school he took his first job as a clerk with a stock exchange firm in London until he went into business with his brother, Louis, in the 1880s. They were extremely successful because the Egyptian bond market was a lucrative endeavor for many English investors at the time. As most English gents of the time did, they traded exclusively in Egyptian bonds and held Egyptian Tribute Loan Stock. Life was good for Gerald and no doubt thought he was set for life. His lofty dreams of living in grandeur ended in January 1885 when the market collapsed, and he and Louis lost it all—some reports claimed millions. Gerald's youngest brother, Godfrey, later wrote, *"…it was the failure of Louis and Gerald who had been on their own account as jobbers that caused all three to decide on trying California."*

When they arrived at the bustling port of Liverpool, the weather was about fifty degrees, the winds were slight, and the skies were clear. By the early nineteenth century, forty percent of the world's trade passed through Liverpool. The docks were abuzz with passengers, crew members, family members, horses, carts, wagon, and steamer trunks all waiting for the White Star Line's next voyage. The *Britannic* was an imposing luxury liner that weighed five thousand and four tons and measured four hundred and fifty-five feet long. Not only was she a steamship but was also fitted with sails and had a large open deck. Ethel and the boys were some of the two hundred and twenty saloon class passengers. This ship steerage capacity was one thousand five-thousand, but only eight hundred were booked on this journey. Their captain was Hamilton Perry who was a true mariner and had come from a long line of seafarers. He was an agreeable man when his time was free, but not when he was busy being the captain. Edward Smith was his second officer, who later became captain of the doomed *Titanic.*

Once everyone was loaded and their trunks stowed, the horns bellowed, the ropes were untied, and *Britannic* pulled of out the harbor. Her passengers were on their way to America and were among the over three hundred forty-five thousand citizens who immigrated to the America that year.

Ethel worried about losing her "Englishness" after being in America and after only being on the ship for six days she wrote, *"I am so afraid that I shall get that American sing-song voice. I have caught myself doing it once or twice already. It is fearfully catching."*

S.S. Britannic, ca. 1884.

Ice Cream Soda

Gerald and the boys spent a large portion of their free time on-board S.S. *Britannic* in the smoking saloon where they enjoyed cigars, pipes, drinking, playing cards, and conversing with the other men. It's here where they likely met a man Ethel referred to as "Mr. D." They were happy to make his acquaintance because he was associated with Northern California. His knowledge of the area was of great interest to them, and like dry sponges on a wet surface, they soaked in all the advice Mr. D. was willing to offer. He shared suggestions on where they should go once they arrived in California. He warned Gerald and his brothers about getting caught up in gold fever or settling in the Antelope Valley, which was a mining town resembling the Sahara Desert. He recommended they go farther north to the foothills. After much consideration, they decided to head to San Francisco, largely in part because the British Consulate had an office where agents could offer them assistance.

On April 26, 1885, Ethel and the boys arrived at Castle Gardens in New York City, and after an ordeal of unloading their luggage, they hailed a cab and rented a "cheap" hotel. Once settled in, they went in search of train tickets to take them to California and paid a visit to Mr. D., who had a place in the city. Ethel wrote, *"We called on Mr. D., and we were entertained by his housekeeper till he came in. He gave me an American drink, which was truly delicious: cream and soda water flavored with maple syrup and vanilla, iced, of course, everything is iced."* She also noted, *"The common people all wear those absurdly baggy blue trousers like they do in France and Germany. The railway, too, goes straight through the streets without any sort of paling or platforms. In fact, I feel as if I were in Cologne again. Food in New York, and also on board the cars, is awfully drear."*

Serves 1

1 to 3 tablespoons maple syrup, extra for drizzling 1 cup club soda 3/4 cup cream 1 teaspoon vanilla Ice	1. Combine syrup and club soda in a cup or bowl to make your flavored soda. Gently whisk together. The amount of syrup added depends on your taste. 2. Combine the cream and vanilla in a measuring cup or bowl to combine. 3. Pour the mixture into a tall glass filled with ice and top off with the flavored soda. 4. Drizzle additional maple syrup over top. 5. Add a tall spoon and paper straw, and you have one of the nineteenth century's most popular lady's drink.

Strawberries & Whipped Cream

The long train journey that began in New York City ended on May 6, 1885, when they pulled into the San Francisco, California, train station. Ethel had been unable to change her clothes so stepped off the train at her final stop in her week-old dress. She didn't want to wait a moment more, so they left their luggage and trunks behind for the railroad staff to deliver later. They hailed a horse-drawn carriage to take them to the opulent Palace Hotel at the corner of Market and New Montgomery Streets. Ethel, Gerald, Louis, Bernard, and Henry were beginning their life in California in first-class style. Their carriage pulled up to the hotel on its gravel driveway that was surrounded by a courtyard. Ethel marveled at balconied galleries and white marble columns extending from the marble pavement of the Grand Central Court to the lofty opaque glass roof. She was amazed at the sophistication of features and furnishings the Palace Hotel boasted.

It opened in 1875 and was one of California's most luxurious hotels. It was allegedly the largest, costliest, and most luxurious hotel in the world. It cost an outrageous five million dollars to complete and featured seven hundred and fifty-five rooms on seven floors, each room being twenty by twenty with fifteen-foot-high ceilings. There were forty-five public and utility rooms, and guests enjoyed the seven thousand windows in the majestic hotel that was hailed as the "Grande Dame of the West." Fifteen marble companies supplied over eight hundred fireplace mantels, nine hundred washbasins, and forty-thousand square feet of flooring, which also included rare woods. Ethel and the boys enjoyed the modern conveniences of the Palace that included five redwood paneled hydraulic elevators, which were reputedly the first in the West, electric call buttons in each room, plumbing and private toilets, shared baths for every two rooms, closets, a telegraph for the staff on each floor, a pneumatic tube system throughout the hotel, air-conditioning, fireplaces, and bay windows in each room.

When Ethel arrived at the hotel at ten in the morning, she had three things on her mind—getting a hot bath, putting on a clean dress, and eating a decadent meal. She immediately went to her room and took her much-needed bath. After enjoying a luxurious soak, Ethel was anxious to put on a clean dress and feel like a proper Victorian lady again. Unbeknownst to the soaking Ethel, her luggage had not arrived yet because of a train mix up. She refused to put her soiled dress back on, so she stayed in her room until her luggage arrived around four p.m. Since she had no clothes, she couldn't leave the room. Not only did she have to wait for a dress, but she was also unable to eat. She wrote, *"I was rather hungry by then."*

Ethel settled into the Palace and was once again enjoying her life as a socialite. She wrote, "Breakfast is always begun with a huge plate of strawberries and cream. The cherries are enormous, and so is the asparagus and many other vegetables." With a renewed spirit, Ethel set out to enjoy her stay at the Palace. She and Gerald ventured into the marble courtyard where they sat in the rocking chairs and discussed their future. One day they visited the British Consulate and spoke with George Edward Stanley, who advised that the Immigration Society could help them. Upon their return, she penned a letter home from the Palace. *"Here we are in the lap of luxury. I never was in such a splendid and enormous hotel in my life."*

Makes 2 Cups

2 cups strawberries, hulled and halved 2 cups whipping cream 1/3 cup sugar	1. Beat the whipping cream in a large bowl with an electric mixer at high speed. Add the sugar and beat until soft peaks form. Serve the strawberries alongside the cream. You can skip the whipping and just sprinkle sugar on the berries and pour cream over them.

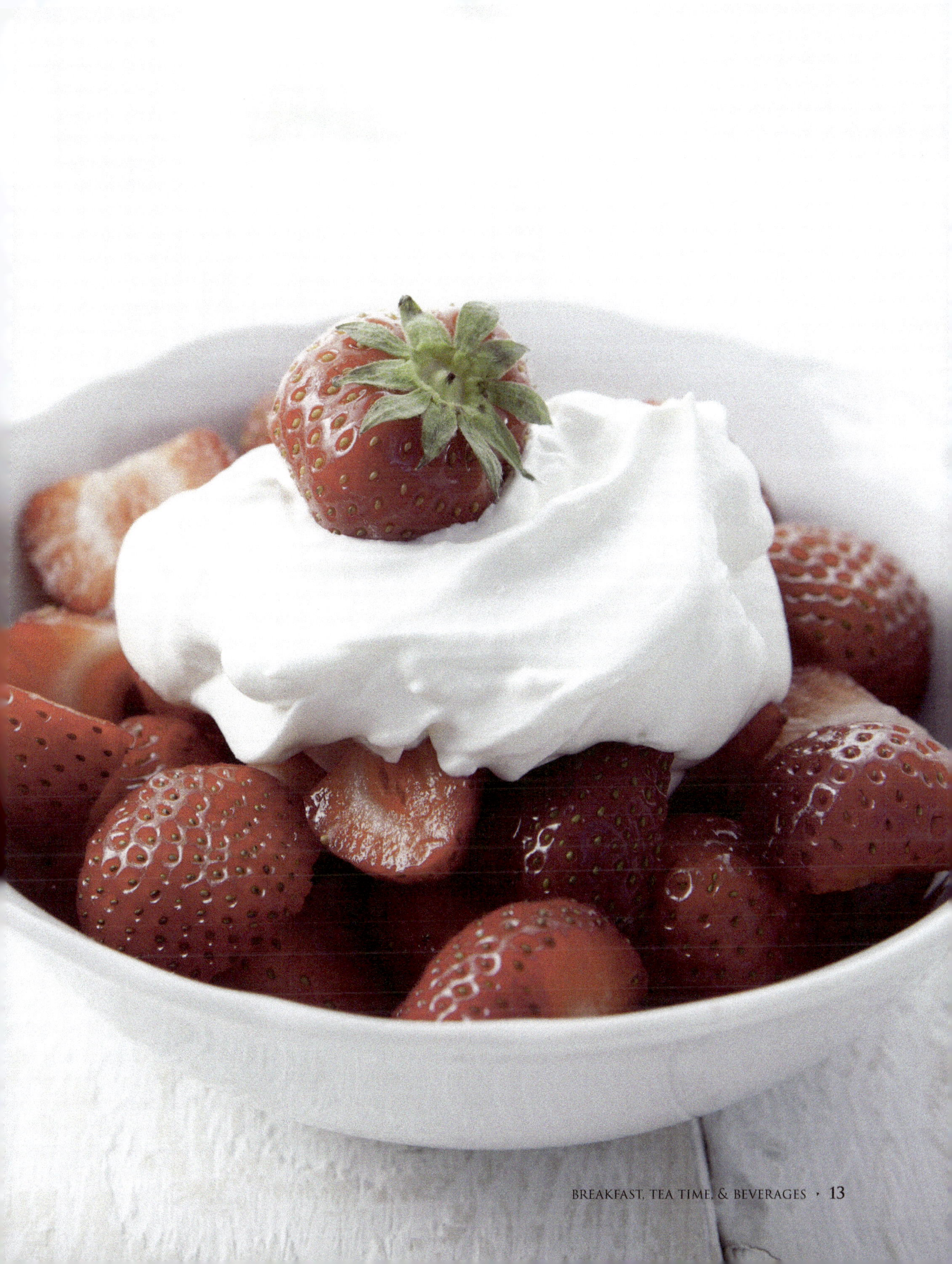

White Bread

With their westward travel accommodations settled, Ethel and Gerald boarded a luxurious Pullman car, and the boys settled into their first-class carriage. Pullman cars had been around for nearly twenty years by the time Ethel had traveled in hers. They were moving luxury hotels and wealthy Victorian passengers like Ethel and Gerald were called "varnish" by the railroad staff because of the opulent wood-grain interiors the Pullman afforded. Passengers like Ethel marveled at the murals on the ceiling, crystal chandeliers, marble countertops in the bathroom, and exotic rugs that covered the floors. The cars included double windows and a patented ventilation system that provided fresh air without train soot. Ethel enjoyed the Pullman car except for the hot pipes under the seats and recalled, "…we feel as if we are sitting on the kitchen stove…."

As the train chugged its way toward Chicago, a heavy downpour caused it to struggle with steep inclines. The train normally ran about twelve miles per hour, but it slowed and crawled toward the top. Heavy rains caused it to jerk suddenly and slip backward. The conductor attempted to climb two more times while Ethel and the other passengers were thrown back and forth. He finally made it over, but Ethel wrote while onboard, *"It's a wonder they don't request us all to get out and walk!"* Because of the delay, Ethel and the boys only had twenty minutes to get off the train, race to the restaurant, dine, and get back. Many train stations did not have restaurants on site, but there was usually one nearby referred to as the emigrants' restaurant. Atchison, Topeka, and Santa Fe railroad man Fred Harvey began to improve train travel food because of the inconsistent and awful food in these emigrant restaurants. Ethel and the boys dashed through the pouring rain and hurriedly ate a quick meal of soup, chicken, beef, two types of dessert, and tea. They dashed back with bread and apples in their hands just in time to catch their train. The meal for all five of them only cost a dollar and a half because they were mistaken for a theatrical troupe. Ethel commented they should keep that "pleasant delusion" up because it got them a discount.

Steam locomotive and passenger cars, ca. 1885.

Makes 1 Loaf

1/4 cup buttermilk

1/4 cup butter, melted

2 eggs, lightly beaten

1/4 cup water

2 tablespoons sugar

1 package rapid or instant yeast

1 teaspoon salt

3 to 3 1/2 cups bread flour

2 teaspoons butter, melted

1. In a large bowl, combine the buttermilk, butter, eggs, water, and sugar.
2. Combine the yeast, salt, and 3 cups of the flour and add to the buttermilk mixture. Mix well and add enough flour to form a soft but not sticky dough.
3. Knead on a floured surface for about 10 minutes. You will know that you have kneaded enough when you press a finger in the dough and it bounces back.
4. Place the dough in a lightly oiled bowl, turn to coat the surface, and cover with a towel or plastic wrap. Allow the dough to double in size in a warm place, about 1 hour.
5. Remove the dough from the bowl and roll into a rectangular shape on a floured surface. Starting at the shortest end, roll the dough up like a jelly roll. Tuck the ends under and place in a greased 9-inch loaf pan. Allow this to rise under a towel in a warm place until doubled.
6. Once the dough has risen again, brush the top with the melted butter and bake at 375°F for 30 minutes.
7. Remove the bread from the pan and cool on a cake rack before slicing.

AN ENGLISH COMMUNITY IN CALIFORNIA

Ethel's husband, Gerald Hertslet ca. 1880.

Until they moved to Lower Lake, Ethel was able to avoid cooking, but once on their own, she had to dive into the dreaded domestic service. Gerald and his brothers chose Lake County for its beautiful climate and hopeful prospects but also because of the current residents living in nearby Burns Valley. The area more closely resembled an English countryside village rather than a western ranching community. An Englishman named Charles Owens formed the Burns Valley Colony Company and invested and settled on the land which was part of the Guenoc Ranch area in 1885. It was a unique community where most of the laborers practiced occasional farming and were sons or nephews of titled Englishmen. Colony residents lived a luxurious lifestyle and enjoyed yachting, coaching, private theatricals, and cricket. It was perfect for the Hertslets—or so they thought.

Gerald eventually created a List of Englishmen Owning Land in and around Lower Lake, which not only listed the landowner's name, but their father's name and position and the total number of acres they owned in Lower Lake. It included a Who's Who of England with names like George Forbes, son of General Sir John Forbes, Knight Grand Cross, Order of the Bath (G.C.B.), and Guy Molesworth. Gerald felt that Ethel would be happy here with people from her own country. He penned a letter home, *"…however, I sincerely hope we shall be able to buy land here, it will be so jolly for Ethel if she can be near these English ladies."* As Gerald had hoped, she immediately felt at home because of the large population of about thirty or so English residents in the area. Burns Valley included the land that sat just outside of Lower Lake and had several large vineyards and fruit farms. While they knew they wanted to settle in the Burns Valley, they were still looking for the perfect spot to put down figurative and literal roots. As they searched for the land that would make them rich, they moved in with one of the English families in the area. Despite having a full house already, sheep ranchers Richard and Effie Keatinge hosted Ethel, Gerald, and Louis. In addition to the Hertslets, the Keatinges had two little boys, Richard Harte and Percy Ridgley, and Effie's sister, Miss May Mitchel. During her time there, Ethel became good friends with Effie and her sister May. His brother Bernard and Henry Brandram stayed with Richard's bachelor brother.

Rock Cakes

They finally settled in Lower Lake in Lake County, California. It's a small town located on Clear Lake in Lake County and just over one hundred miles north of San Francisco. It lies between the Mayacamas and Bear Mountains, and the center of the valley, which is Clear Lake, is twenty-five miles long with an average width of seven miles. It's divided into two parts, Upper and Lower Lake, the two being connected by a strait known as The Narrows. While more than half of the county was covered with rugged mountains and water, the balance consisted of foothill and valley lands, which were exceedingly fertile. While in Lower Lake, the brothers met up with affluent Guy Molesworth, who educated them on life in the area. He was a fellow Brit and son of Sir Guilford Molesworth, who was Knight Commander Most Eminent Order of the Indian Empire (K.C.I.E.).

Once they found the right land, they began building while they lived nearby with Rowland Brown. While the men were busy building the house and digging the well for the new home, Ethel grew lonely. Day after day of cleaning, cooking, and washing had worn her down, and she suffered depression like many frontier women did. While they lived at Mr. Brown's, she wrote a letter to her best friend Rose back in England. *"Of course the boys, coming back after working and joking together all day, don't understand my being depressed and think I am discontented."* To help alleviate her loneliness, she got a companion dog who reminded her of her old dog Vixen she had back in England. She enjoyed Rags the ranch dog, and his antics made her laugh, especially when it was hot. She giggled when he sat in the pig's drinking trough with only his head out of the water for hours. The heat remained intolerable her first summer and continued to surpass the one-hundred-degree mark in the kitchen by nine o'clock in the morning. The washing was the bane of her life, and she noted, *"It is no joke in this hot weather."*

Day after day of oppressive heat, being overwhelmed with chores and alone pushed Ethel to take an afternoon off. She decided to go calling on some of the nearby English ladies for some desperately needed socializing. After she prepared the afternoon dinner, she washed up and decided the boys were on their own for supper. She didn't want to completely abandon them, so she baked them a huge pile of rock cakes, which are better known as English drop scones. She saddled up Mr. Brown's horse and went directly to nearby neighbors, Richard and Effie Keatinge, where she enjoyed a supper she didn't have to prepare. Later that evening, the Keatinges had a party where about twenty of the British gentry gathered. Gerald also joined them, and he and Ethel sang songs with the group. She penned, *"…we sang songs (they like Gerald's and my singing so much)."*

Makes About 12

1 1/2 cups flour	1. Place the flour in a large mixing bowl and add the baking powder. Add the butter and stir until all the lumps are gone.
2 teaspoons baking powder	
1/2 cup butter, melted	2. Add the currants, nutmeg, sugar, and candied peel and mix well. Add the egg and milk mixture and stir well. The batter will be stiff.
1 cup currants or raisins	
1 teaspoon grated nutmeg or ginger	3. Grease a cookie sheet with butter. Divide the dough into small portions and place on a cookie sheet. Put them in a cold oven and then set the temperature to 240°F and bake for about 15 minutes.
1/2 cup sugar	
2 ounces candied lemon or orange peel, cut into pieces	4. Serve with Jam or whipped cream.
1 egg, beaten with 1/4 cup milk	

Currant Loaf

Ethel began her American journey in 1885 with her husband Gerald when they arrived in New York City, and some twenty years later, her life had completely changed. She was divorced and now with her cousin and life partner, Claude Barry. Ethel met up with Claude in Montreal, Canada, when she returned and began acting again under the name of Ethel Hertslet at the Theatre Francais. Even though she no longer considered herself Mrs. Hertslet, she had already established herself as an actor under that name, and changing it would be like starting all over again. In October, she and Claude moved to the booming city of New York where her current manager, Mr. Wright, was forming a new company and had a new play where Ethel would have the lead. She even copyrighted her own five-act drama called, *The Silence of Dean Maitland*.

Once in Manhattan, Mr. and Mrs. Claude Barry leased a modest brick building called the Hospitality House at 145 E. 49th Street from Anthony Ballind. Ethel's acting career was all set, or so she thought, but her manager failed, and she was out of a job with no prospects. Claude hoped to hire on as an accountant in a firm like he had in San Francisco but had no luck. Manhattan was a large city teeming with people looking for a job, and Ethel believed that was another reason why Claude hadn't secured a position. Claude was stunned that people with their intelligence, energy, and talent couldn't find work in the six weeks they looked. He said, "My wife is a clever actress… looked for other engagements, and I answered advertisement after advertisement." Days turned into weeks, and their money melted away. Claude was brought to tears with pride as he watched Ethel proudly manage their household on a tight budget.

In the beginning, Ethel and Claude walked everywhere to save cab fare. Sometimes her strolls took her to Canal Street, which was an hour-long walk from her apartment. Claude did the same—both in search of work and errands. At the end of the day, they both headed to their apartment, each hoping the other had good news. Neither did. Their once buoyant and cheerful attitude was nearing extinction. Ethel eventually found work but not as an actress. She worked as a photo tinter but was required to buy her own equipment that cost almost four dollars. The firm she worked for supplied the photos with the glass on which they were to be mounted, and she was promised twenty-five cents for each dozen she completed. She thought there was hope and began tinting. She quickly learned that it was no easy task, and even the smallest air bubble would ruin the photo. She recalled, "It is maddening to try anything so delicate when you are excessively nervous. Well, I ruined more than I could make ten times over, and I gave it up."

When reporter Sibyl Wilbur of New York City's *The World* learned of their challenges, she convinced Ethel and Claude to share their story. Once the story ran, strangers showed up at their door with all sorts of goodies. One was a street car conductor and his wife who brought them stuffed chickens, freshly baked bread, and butter and jelly. He told them he had fallen on hard times in the past and understood their plight. Claude was given a position as an accountant with an esteemed firm, and Ethel received engagements from at least seven different stage managers. She was teary-eyed at the generosity of people and said, "This experience has taught us both that the world is full of kind hearts if one can only reach them."

During the lean times, they formed a plan and followed Miss Banks's three dollars a week plan that she outlined in the *Evening World*. In fact, they did better than Miss Banks. They didn't know where she did her shopping, but they visited stores on Second and Third Avenues where they found bargains. The month of January was rough indeed, and their meals consisted of minimal items. One day they ate mutton stew and bread and another consisted of bread, currant loaf, coffee, and butter. They usually had "meat" along with butter, bread, milk, or coffee. Ethel stated that beefsteak was beyond their means and pork made them ill.

Makes 1 Loaf

2 tablespoons butter, softened 1 cup sugar 1 large egg 1 1/2 cups whole milk 2 cups flour 1 teaspoon baking powder 1 cup currants	1. Cream the butter and sugar together in a large bowl. Add the egg and the milk and mix well. Gradually add the flour and baking powder and mix until combined. Dust the currants with flour and stir into the batter. 2. Pour into a greased 9 x 5-inch loaf pan. Bake at 350°F for 55 to 60 minutes or until a toothpick inserted in the center comes out clean. Cool for 10 minutes before removing from pan to a wire rack.

Note: You can also use a combination of raisins, currants, or other similar dried fruit.

Sourdough Bread

When Ethel penned letters home in 1885 and 1886 from her California ranch, she often described her cooking and the meals she prepared. It's not surprising because she never cooked before and seemed pleased with her ability to adapt and create tasty meals. Her bread was her most impressive accomplishment. *"I made a splendid batch of bread the day we came, eight good-sized loaves, and they are all gone in two days! My bread is very good, which is rather a drawback, as they eat much more of it. Besides the bother of making bread, we have to make the yeast here about once a week."* Ethel soon learned how to handle sourdough and made her starter with potatoes, hops, salt, and sugar. The local ladies who taught her how to make it recalled, "One cupful of old yeast is put in to start the new batch, which is then put to rise in a large stone jar in a cool place." She also realized that sourdough was temperamental and needed to be maintained. When she accidentally ran out, she relied on her neighbors and wrote, *"The yeast, though, is a trial. We got some from the Keatinges on Sunday, but Gerald broke the bottle coming up here; then he went to the Beakebanes for some, and that wouldn't ferment properly and took thirty-six hours to rise, by which time I had given it up and got some more from Mrs. C., which at last is a fine success, and the shelf of my store-room is swamped with it."* It's best to weigh the flour when making this bread.

Makes 1 Loaf

4 ounces sourdough starter 12 ounces water, not warm 1 pound 4 ounces bread flour 1/2 ounce salt (non-iodized)	1. Combine the sourdough starter and water into a bowl and stir. Add the flour and salt and blend with a spoon or dough mixer until incorporated and a little stiff. Next, using your hands, mix the dough together to form a ball and incorporate all the ingredients together but do not knead. 2. Place a little oil in the bowl and place the dough back in it and cover. Allow it to rise until it has doubled in size, which should be about 12 hours depending on the room's temperature. Once the dough has doubled, gently remove it from the bowl and do not deflate. Sprinkle the work surface with a little flour, but not too much, and then flour your hands. Shape the dough and place it into a greased Dutch oven or loaf pan. Cover and let it rise on the countertop for 90 minutes. Place into a cold oven and turn the oven to 425°F and bake, covered, for 45 minutes. Remove the lid and bake for an additional 15 minutes. 3. Remove from the pan and allow to cool completely before slicing.

Scrambled Eggs

Being in charge of meals meant Ethel no longer had the luxury of sleeping in. She had to rise between five thirty and six each morning to cook breakfast for the men. Some days she made porridge, while other days she made eggs. Fortunately, Rowland Brown's farm produced an abundant amount of milk, butter, and eggs. She did, however, need to get additional amounts of food staples, but they did not come cheaply. A pound of pounded white sugar cost four dollars. They could have purchased unpounded, but that would have required someone to take a hatchet to it. Two hundred pounds of flour was a little more reasonable at six dollars a barrel.

She prepared all the meals for the men on Mr. Brown's ranch including afternoon tea. Since the men were away in town, she was left to chop firewood for the stove and then lit it just enough to boil water. She then set about preparing for the afternoon ritual. She decided to make scrambled eggs to go with the tea because she didn't want to stoke up the stove and bake in the heat. She had no idea how to make the eggs, so she reached for one of her cookbooks. She later remarked, *"I had not a ghost of an idea how it was going to turn out, but it was quite a success."* Even though she had many clippings, she often referred to English cookbooks like this one, *Lessons in Cookery, Hand-book of the National Training School for Cookery.*

Serves 4-6

8 eggs	1. Beat the eggs in a bowl and set aside.
3/4 cup cream	2. Put the cream and butter together in a small saucepan and heat over low heat until the butter melts. Remove from the heat. Add the eggs into the cream and sprinkle with the salt and pepper.
8 tablespoons butter	
1 teaspoon salt	
1/2 teaspoon pepper	
	3. Place the pan back over medium heat and whisk with a fork until the eggs begin to firm.
	4. Serve at once.

Curried Eggs

Ethel and Gerald officially took possession of their ranch on July 28, 1885, after Gerald, Louis, and Bernard purchased eighty acres of Rowland Brown's farm. Day by day, Ethel's house neared completion, and the ranch was taking shape. The week before she moved in, her recently ordered stove arrived. She was quite pleased with it, despite not knowing what to do with half of the things it included. They placed the stove in the kitchen so it stood out in the room and could be walked around. It came equipped with six large holes on the top that had lids, a boiler, and a large oven. It also included two large stock pots, a large boiler for clothes, three types of frying pans, a gridiron, a tea kettle, and a variety of baking tins. It also included another item which confounded the novice cook Ethel. *"…and a large saucepan with holes all over the bottom. I cannot imagine the use of it."* Ethel planned a dinner for seven local bachelors and once again pulled out her cookbooks and flipped through them to choose her menu, and one of the items she served was curried eggs.

Serves 2-4

4 tablespoons butter 2 onions, sliced 1 tablespoon curry powder 2 tablespoons flour 1 cup of cream or vegetable stock 6 hard-boiled eggs, halved Salt and pepper, to taste	1. Melt the butter in a frying pan over medium heat until golden in color. Add the curry powder and flour and stir for about 1 minute. Stir in the cream or stock until combined and simmer for 10 minutes. Taste for seasoning. Add the eggs and simmer for about 5 minutes and serve. You could also use poached eggs and just pour the sauce over them.

Apple Jelly

Fall had come to Lake County, California, and Ethel bought ninety-seven pounds of apples to make apple jelly for the winter. Her neighbor, Miss May, arrived unexpectedly to help her, and Ethel was in the middle of ironing. Ethel was not prepared to make jelly at this moment, but Miss May advised this was the best time for her as she was busy and would not be able to come back. Ethel, never having made apple jelly before, was at the mercy of Miss May's last-minute calling. Putting her ironing aside, she prepared to make jelly for the first time. They began by stewing the apples to make a pulp and then strained them through flour sacks to get the juice. They then rubbed the strained pulp through a sieve so they could make jam from it. Ethel was quite pleased with her first attempt. *"The jelly is lovely and is a beautiful red color, though the apples were quite green. And my hands are shocking! The apples have stained them black. It was a tiring day… excepting my meals, I never sat down from 7:30 a.m. to 7:30 p.m."*

Makes 4 to 5 Pints

6 pounds of red and green apples to get 4 cups apple juice 2 tablespoons lemon juice 3 cups sugar	1. Wash, de-stem, and cut the bottom blossom ends off the apples but do not peel. Cut apples into small pieces and place in a stockpot. Add water, cover, and bring to a boil on high heat. Reduce heat and simmer for 20 to 25 minutes or until apples are soft. 2. Strain the apples through double thick cheesecloth, a jelly bag strainer, or clean tea towel over a colander. Squeeze until enough juice is extracted. 3. Mix the apple juice, lemon, and sugar into a large stock pot and boil over high heat. Cook at high heat, stirring constantly, until the gelling point is reached, which is 220°F. 4. Ladle jelly into sterilized jars leaving a 1/4-inch headspace. Wipe rims clean and screw on the lids. Process for 10 minutes in water bath canner (add 1 minute for every 1,000 feet above sea level).

Note: Ethel kept the strained pulp and made a jam, but it could also be made into a spread.

Port Wine Jelly

The New Year of 1886 started very cold, with frozen pipes and a missing cow. Even though Ethel loved her cow, she was miffed when she ran off because that meant no milk, cream, or butter. Because of Becky's constant disappearing acts, they soon bought a new cow. Louis found a three-year-old cow, who cost thirty dollars ($702), and was expecting a calf in July. When Becky did arrive back home, she was pregnant, so Ethel would have another calf. Life on the ranch ebbed and flowed with routine work and unexpected events. After the summer heat, Ethel and Burns Valley welcomed the coolness of winter. However, the extreme cold was shocking to her. Their wooden house didn't hold the heat very well, and spilled tea immediately froze to the table. Despite the weather, they celebrated Gerald's birthday on January 6 with the Keatinges and savored a turkey dinner, plum pudding, and port wine jelly. This is the ranch house where Ethel, Gerald, Louis, Bernard, and Henry Brandram lived until they moved away in the 1890s.

Makes 4 Pints

4 cups port wine 1/2 cup lemon juice 6 cups granulated sugar 6 ounces liquid fruit pectin	1. Place the wine, lemon juice, and sugar in a large pot and bring to a boil over high heat. Stir slowly and constantly with a large spoon. Boil for 1 minute. 2. Remove from the heat and slowly stir in pectin and blend well. 3. Ladle jelly into sterilized jars leaving a 1/4-inch headspace. Wipe rims clean and screw on the lids. Process for 10 minutes in water bath canner (add 1 minute for every 1,000 feet above sea level).

The Hertslet Ranch, with the family visible on the house's front porch, ca. 1886..

THE TRUTH BEGINS TO SHOW

Gerald frequently changed his mind about what to plant on their California ranch. The Hertslet men abandoned plans to plant 100% vines, opting instead to fence twenty acres—half for vines, half for hay. They also expanded their poultry collection, buying seven turkeys, six hens, and one "gobbler," as they called the cock. Gerald told Ethel turkeys were profitable, worth as much as sheep, and easy to care for.

As their ranch house was being built, they debated income-earning ventures. Having never farmed a day in their lives, their decisions often reflected ignorance. They began poultry farming with one hen laying thirteen eggs, quickly adding thirteen chickens. Though chickens provided income, they were companions for Ethel, who adored all the ranch animals, writing, *"My little chickens are so sweet."* Coyotes, hawks, and pigs plagued their flock, prompting them to keep the chickens cooped. Ethel wasn't pleased that turkeys fought her beloved chickens. The family also considered olive trees but balked at the four-year wait for fruit. Gerald's restless nights, which Ethel attributed to exhaustion, included dreams of chasing chickens.

In the summer of 1886, their water tank tipped over, dooming four acres of alfalfa and forcing Gerald and his brothers to water olive trees by hand until they gave up, leaving them to dry and fall prey to wandering cows. Deciding fencing was too costly, they committed fully to chicken ranching, envisioning a lucrative operation. With 22 hens, two cocks, and several broods, they sold ten eggs a day for thirty cents per dozen. They hoped eventually to scale up to 200 hens and even considered a $70 incubator. Gerald wrote home about their ambition, lamenting the lack of capital but vowing to persevere.

Challenges mounted: skunks raided the henhouse, hawks picked off chickens, and Gerald mistakenly poisoned five hens with tinned mackerel. Winter cold killed over 200 chicks, first from faulty coal lamps, then from exposure when lamps were removed. Despite setbacks, they briefly ventured into honey bees, buying three hives. Lacking expertise, they mishandled the bees, which grew aggressive and stung indiscriminately. Gerald's attempt to kill the bees with chemicals ruined the honey, as well.

With failed ventures piling up, Gerald's brother Louis took a break to housesit for a friend deep in the woods. Before leaving, they spent an evening on the verandah, singing the melancholy "Jack's Yarn," its verse foreshadowing their struggles: *"And no more luck was traveling about."*

Gerald Hertslet's brother, Louis Hertslet, ca. 1880.

BREAKFAST, TEA TIME, & BEVERAGES · 25

Apricot Jam

Ethel wanted her Lake County home to be as refined as her English one. Before leaving England, she packed a lovely English breakfast service, including delicate porcelain cups, saucers, and plates. To save on freight costs, she decided to order a dinner and glass service once settled. As their home neared completion, Ethel and Henry rode into Lower Lake, where she scoured catalogs but was dismayed to find that five pounds in California would only buy a thick, clunky white set, far inferior to what she could get in England. Despite her disappointment, she placed an order for a dinner and glass service from a San Francisco company. However, the money sent with the order was stolen. She wrote home in late June, *"Isn't it enraging? The money we sent to San Francisco for our dinner service and glass has been stolen on the way. It was sent in greenbacks and not registered, so we have no redress."*

Fortunately, her coveted breakfast set survived the journey, arriving almost a month later with only a few broken items. Another trunk contained her washing dresses and cooking aprons, a welcome relief as she had been doing housework in her impractical Victorian day dresses. After paying for her new items, Ethel purchased staples, including twenty-five pounds of apricots for one dollar to make jam. She passed on blackberries, finding them too expensive.

On the bumpy road home, Ethel noticed Rags chasing something. Picking up their pace, they saw the dog drive a skunk directly into the wagon wheels. The skunk sprayed them in defense, with Henry getting the worst of it. He took a bath as soon as they returned home.

Around this time, someone suggested Ethel write a book about her adventures in America. Thrilled by the idea, she wrote, *"I think it would be a capital idea to make a little book of our adventures. It would give a good idea to intending emigrants in our class of life of what they will have to put up with."*

Makes 5-6 Pints

4 to 4 1/2 cups of ripe, crushed apricots 4 cups sugar 2 tablespoons lemon juice	1. Wash and rinse the apricots before cooking. Peel and remove the pits and then cut into pieces. Crush the fruit and measure. Place the apricots, sugar, and lemon juice into a large pot and bring to a boil while stirring constantly. Cook at high heat until the gelling point is reached, which is 220°F. 2. Ladle jam into sterilized jars leaving a 1/4-inch headspace. Wipe rims clean and screw on the lids. Process for 5 minutes in water bath canner (add 1 minute for every 1,000 feet above sea level).

Peach Jam

On one of her trips into Lower Lake, she visited her green grocer, Peter de Lucci, where Ethel procured seventy pounds of unripe peaches to make jam. While Ethel was not impressed with the stores, she felt differently about her green grocer's name when she penned home, *"Isn't that an aristocratic name!"* It was here where she bought produce like potatoes.

Makes 6-7 Pints

5 1/2 to 6 cups of ripe, crushed peaches 4 to 5 cups sugar 2 tablespoons lemon juice	1. Sterilize jars and lids and according to the manufacturer's directions. 2. Wash and rinse the peaches before cooking. Peel and remove the pits and then cut into pieces. Crush the fruit and measure. Place the peaches, sugar, and lemon juice into a large pot and bring to a boil while stirring constantly. Cook at high heat until the gelling point is reached, which is 220°F. 3. Ladle jam into sterilized jars leaving a 1/4-inch headspace. Wipe rims clean and screw on the lids. Process for 5 minutes in water bath canner (add 1 minute for every 1,000 feet above sea level).

REVIEW OF ETHEL'S NEW BOOK

Frontispiece from Ethel's Ranch Life in California, *titled "Our Ranch."*

Since farming didn't work out for him, Gerald, along with his friend Thomas Beakbane, turned back to their white-collar roots. They set up an insurance, loan, and real estate business. Because of these two men, a great change took place in the lower Clear Lake surroundings and especially in the Burns Valley. They set up a real estate office in town, and Gerald stayed at the local headquarters while Beakbane spent a good part of his time in England. He sold the idea to wealthy prospective buyers looking for an investment, especially to farm. Their first advertisement ran in San Francisco in October. They wrote that the land in Lake County was not only healthy but also picturesque. They also tried to attract other Brits to purchase, and they noted there was a large English community already established there. They later modified their advertising to claim that the area was the Little Switzerland of America.

While Gerald was busy trying to sell real estate, Ethel had finished her book, and it was released in late 1886. One reviewer in *Lloyd's Weekly* newspaper wrote: *"Three brothers whose sole experience of life was a superficial knowledge of the Stock Exchange business; the wife of the eldest; and a 'mutual friend' left England for California in the spring of 1885, with a total capital of 500£. [pounds], to buy a piece of land, build a house, and stock the farm; all bent on doing their level best to thrive. The letters of Evelyn, the refined and well-domesticated lady of the party, which make up the book, range over a year and a half of intense hard work, and show clearly that without experience and capital, a fortune it not easier of attainment in the 'Golden State' than in this country. Rather than start with only 100£., this lady considers a man would be infinitely better off to go as a day labourer with nothing. There are bright and cheerful passages, however; evil fortunes are borne with constancy; and none of the party seem to have expected the results of labour, without the labour."*

This review called out the Hertslet's multiple failures and likely did not sit well with them. Sir Edward Hertslet, who was also not pleased, had been funding most of their time in Burns Valley, along with Ethel's allowance. Their youngest, Godfrey, who did not go to California, later wrote, *"…they must have had a pretty good time while the money (supplied by father) lasted."*

28 · VICTORIAN RECIPES WITH A SIDE OF SCANDAL

Marmalade Tartlets

These were just two of the many desserts that Ethel was offered aboard the S.S. *Britannic* during her journey to America in 1885.

Makes About 40 2-Inch Tarts

2 cups flour 1 1/4 cups cold butter, cut into pieces 2 teaspoons sugar 1/2 cup cold water 1 cup orange marmalade	1. Rub the butter into the flour, then add the sugar and the water. Mix well until the dough comes together. This can also be done in a food processor, but do not over pulse the dough, just until it forms a ball. Refrigerate for 1 hour to chill the butter. Roll it out into a rectangle about 12 x 18-inch. Fold the dough over in thirds, like a letter to be put in an envelope, and roll out again. Dust with flour as needed. Do this four times to build flaky layers. Refrigerate again for 45 minutes. 2. Remove half the dough from the refrigerator and roll out to a 1/4-inch thickness and cut into desired shapes to fit tartlet molds or muffin tins. Do the same with the remaining chilled dough. Place about a teaspoon of jelly or about half-way up in the dough. 3. Bake at 350°F for 25 to 30 minutes until lightly golden and the marmalade is set.

Cheesecake Tarts

Makes About 12 Tarts

8 ounces cream cheese, softened 1 tablespoon butter, softened 1/2 cup sugar 1 egg 1 teaspoon vanilla Puff pastry or pie crust, unbaked	1. Combine the cream cheese and butter in a bowl and beat to combine. Add the sugar and mix until blended. Add the egg and vanilla and beat until mixed. 2. Scoop into tart molds or muffin tins lined with unbaked puff pastry or unbaked pie crusts. 3. Bake at 350°F for about 20 to 25 minutes or until set. Allow to cool before serving. 4. If using berries, place on top before serving and brush with honey to glaze.

Note: Fresh berries for garnish, optional; honey, for glazing the fruits, also optional.

Apple Jelly Tarts

In November 1885, Ethel wrote they were going to have a dance at the New Hall, and several Americans were coming in from Lower Lake. However, it had to be put off because of rain and the bad condition of the roads. Ethel wrote, *"I made fifty tarts, twenty-five apple jelly and twenty-five cheese-cakes. My puff pastry was very successful, and my tarts look most inviting! We have managed to get rid of them without much trouble."*

Makes About 40 2-Inch Tarts

2 cups flour 1 1/4 cups cold butter, cut into pieces 2 teaspoons sugar 1/2 cup cold water 1 cup apple jelly	1. Rub the butter into the flour, then add the sugar and the water. Mix well until the dough comes together. This can also be done in a food processor, but do not over pulse the dough, just until it forms a ball. Refrigerate for 1 hour to chill the butter. Roll it out into a rectangle about 12 x 18-inches. Fold the dough over in thirds, like a letter to be put in an envelope, and roll out again. Dust with flour as needed. Do this four times to build flaky layers. Refrigerate again for 45 minutes. 2. Remove half the dough from the refrigerator and roll out to a 1/4-inch thickness and cut into desired shapes to fit tartlet molds or muffin tins. Do the same with the remaining chilled dough. Place about a teaspoon of jelly or about half-way up in the dough. 3. Bake at 350°F for 25 to 30 minutes until lightly golden and the jelly is set.

Apple Tart

During her train trip from New York to California, Ethel's patience was tested as their train traversed the hot arid lands of Nevada. It was May 4, 1885, when they stopped in Winnemucca, which was about half-way through Nevada and some four hundred miles into their journey. It was a small town of about seven hundred people with several stores to support them. Several ranches within a two hundred mile radius also relied on Winnemucca for their supplies. Ethel noted, *"Fancy having to drive your team 200 miles to get your groceries, &e.[etc.]! One of the ranches at that distance from the town has 175 men on it doing the work."*

They pulled into the Winnemucca depot, where the train parked for four hours. Ethel and the boys got off and explored the area. The town was trying to give itself an air of sophistication and had recently planted poplar trees. They were the only trees in town and provided some shade, where it was only seventy-eight degrees. They all worked up an appetite after their refreshing swim in the Humboldt, so they went into town and devoured a hearty lunch that cost them each twenty-five cents. They sat down to a meal of soup, two types of meat, potatoes, beans, cabbage, beet root, dessert, and apple tart. It was curious to Ethel how the vegetables were served in their own dish, while the meats were served on one large plate for each person. At most meals, they had about thirty dishes on the table at one time. For the second time since arriving in America, Ethel was impressed with the common use of ice for serving beverages. *"There seems to be an abundance of ice in these parts. In none of our English villages could you get iced water like we do here. This place is in a valley, so like the Rhone valley, with just the same breeze blowing in the middle of the day only."*

After a pleasant day in town, they headed back to the train to write letters home and get them posted before the train departed. It was during this part of her journey when Ethel encountered her first Indian—likely from the Northern Paiute tribe that inhabited the area. The Paiutes had two famous members—Chief Winnemucca, whom the town was named after, and his daughter, Sarah Winnemucca.

Serves 6

1 cup flour 1 teaspoon sugar 1/4 teaspoon salt 6 tablespoons cold butter, cut into small pieces 1/4 cup cold water 3 to 4 apples, peeled, cored, and sliced thin 1 tablespoon butter, for topping 1 tablespoon sugar, for topping	1. Combine the flour with the sugar, salt, and butter in a food processor and process for about 5 seconds or until crumbly. Add the water and pulse for about 5-10 seconds or until the pastry just begins to come together. 2. Lightly sprinkle the work surface with flour and dump the pastry onto it. Gather it together until smooth and pat into a disk. Dust with flour and roll out the pastry until fairly thin and about 12-inches round. Place the dough onto a baking sheet lined with parchment paper or foil. Place the apples over the dough, leaving a 1-inch edge to be folded over onto the apples. Dot the apples with the butter and sugar. Bake at 400°F for about 45 minutes or until the apples are tender and the pastry is golden.

Peach Tart

In 1885, Ethel became pregnant with her first of three children. She managed to keep up with her chores and maintained the ranch household. As supplies dwindled, she hitched up the wagon and headed into Lower Lake along a very rugged, bumpy road. She visited her green Lower Lake grocer again, Peter de Lucchi, where she procured a variety of items, including fresh peaches. Her cow Becky provided her with ample quantities of milk and cream, but they couldn't make butter because of the heat. One day she used some of Becky's cream instead of butter to make pastry for a peach tart for the boys' lunch. She was very pleased with her endeavor.

Serves 6

1 1/2 cups flour 1 cup heavy cream 2 teaspoons sugar 3 to 4 tablespoons water 1 1/2 pounds peaches 2 tablespoons sugar	1. Combine the flour, cream, sugar, and water in a bowl and gently mix until the dough comes together. Roll it to a 1/2-inch thickness. Place crust in the tart pan and place the berries on it and sprinkle with sugar. 2. Pit, peel, and slice the peaches and then place them in a flat pie plate and sprinkle with sugar. Cover with the crust and press a fork around the edges to seal and make a pattern. Sprinkle additional sugar over the top of the crust and bake at 375°F for 30 to 40 minutes or until golden.

Blackberry Tart

Even though Ethel often found the cost of blackberries high in Lower Lake, she managed to make a tart for dessert when she had the Keatinges over for supper.

Serves 6

1 1/2 cups flour 1 cup butter, cut into pieces 1/2 cup water 2 to 3 cups blackberries 2 to 3 tablespoons sugar	1. Rub the butter into the flour, then add the sugar and the water. Mix well until the dough comes together. Roll it out and fold it over; do this three times. Divide the dough in half and chill for 1 hour. Roll out the dough for a bottom and top crust to about 1/4-inch. 2. Place crust in the tart pan or the pie pan and place the berries on it and sprinkle with sugar. Cover with the crust and press a fork around the edges to seal and make a pattern. Sprinkle additional sugar over the top of the crust and bake at 375°F for 25 to 30 minutes until golden.

ETHEL GOES SKINNY DIPPING

While in Winnemucca, they were allowed to get off the train for a while, so Ethel and Gerald went one direction, while Louis, Bernard, and Henry ventured in another. As she and Gerald crossed a bridge over the Humboldt River, they saw some boys swimming and got an idea. Without being able to change her clothes in a week in the continuous heat, Ethel did the unthinkable. She and Gerald triumphantly found a quiet spot down river where only the cows could see them. After stripping off all their clothing, they slipped into the refreshing water. It was heaven, and all her frustrations were washed away, but because the river flowed swiftly, they soon discovered that neither she nor Gerald could touch the bottom. Since they were good swimmers, they weren't concerned, but the current did prove difficult when they tried to get out. Their swim was brief because Ethel was "in mortal fright" of getting caught. This was the Victorian era, and it would have been shameful for Ethel to get caught skinny-dipping! If not for that, she would have stayed in much longer.

Ethel adored animals, so it's not surprising to know that she was amused with the furry little creatures she saw running around on the banks of the river. Ethel had never seen such an animal before. They were cute, little black creatures with white stripes down their backs. She described them as, "…tails like a squirrels', about the size of large rats, and with very pretty little faces." There are no skunks in England, so Ethel had no idea how lucky she was to not have been "welcomed" by them. While Gerald and Ethel wisely sought a secluded swimming spot away from town, Louis, Bernard, and Henry did not. They had the same idea but decided to swim closer to town, which almost got them arrested. When an officer asked them if they were from New York, they told him no—they were from England. He remarked he could hardly believe them, as he said they spoke too well for English, "who all talk with a 'haitch' and a 'ho' and a 'he.'" Ethel thought he was kind to tell the boys they did not talk badly.

Winnemucca, Nevada, ca.1860..

BREAKFAST, TEA TIME & BEVERAGES

Tea

The tea that Ethel and everyone else served was looseleaf and not in the tidy little bags used today. Milk was also important with tea, and Ethel needed her own cow for their new home. In 1885, her husband Gerald and his brother Bernard hitched up a wagon and drove to Sulphur Bank where they bought their first cow named Becky and her calf for fifty dollars. Ethel quickly grew attached to Becky and adored the little curly, white fringe between her horns. She insisted on milking Becky, and Gerald only agreed if she gave up dinner clean-up. Ethel liked taking care of Becky but also felt the burden because she knew she would be more consistent than the boys. Her letter home showed her mixed feelings about it. *"I milk at a quarter to six in the morning, and at the same hour in the evening. It is rather a tire; but I am more likely to be regular than either of the boys...."* She also wrote, *"They all laugh at me because I think so much of my Becky and say I think more of her comfort that I do of theirs!"* Ethel learned how to milk cows when she lived with the Keatinges before settling in their own home. Effie's sister May was her tutor, and her many domestic skills included cooking, milking, and laundry. Ethel began doing things she never imagined and tried her hand at cooking, starching, and ironing. She and May wandered to the barn for a milking lesson, and Ethel was warned the cow became spooked at almost anything. So, Ethel nervously started her lesson and failed miserably, but the next day she tried again and succeeded even though the cow kicked the pail over when she was spooked by a sound. Back in the day, milk was placed into the porcelain cup before the hot tea, so the cup wouldn't shatter.

Serves As Many as You Like

Loose leaf tea Boiling water Milk or Half and half Sugar	1. Place as much loose-leaf tea as you like in a ceramic or glass teapot. Pour boiling water over it and let it steep for about 6 minutes or until desired strength. Serve with half and half and sugar.

Russian Cocktail

As Ethel toiled in the house and the barn, her English "farming" men took frequent weekly convivials and spent more time playing than they did farming. Tales of cricket playing, boating, lazy ranching habits, and an overall good time were conjured up whenever the Hertslets name came up. The cricket matches were known throughout the valley, as were the parties that followed. Gerald was known for mixing a mean cocktail back in England, and now in Burns Valley, and was renowned for his gin fizzes and Russian cocktails. As popular as this cocktail was, there is only one historic "recipe" for it, and there are no proportions, so this is an improvisation. The San Francisco newspaper claimed it was originally called the Buck and Breck, referring to 1856 U.S. presidential candidates James Buchanan and John C. Breckinridge. A guide to making the cocktail appeared in the *San Francisco Examiner* in 1888 and is very similar to William "Cocktail" Boothby's version in his 1908 bartender guide.

Serves 1

Crushed ice Granulated sugar Dashes Angostura bitters 1 1/2 ounces VSOP Cognac Twisted lemon peel Champagne or other sparkling wine	1. Fill a champagne glass with ice and swirl it around to moisten and chill the glass. Dump the ice out. Coat the inside of the glass with sugar. Turn the glass upside down and tap the bottom to remove any loose sugar. 2. Add a couple dashes of bitters around the inside of the glass, add the cognac, and a twist of lemon peel. Top with Champagne and serve.

This is the Hertslet and Beakbane boat on Clear Lake. ca 1880s.

Gin Fizz

This and the Russian cocktail were the trendy drinks of the day in northern California in the 1880s, and according to a *San Francisco Chronicle* account of Gerald's life in Lake County, they reported, *"Gerald's gin fizzes were unsurpassed, and his Russian cocktails simply ecstatic."*

In fact, one June night in 1886, Ethel, Louis, and Edith were abruptly woken by a loud crash at four in the morning. Poor Edith thought it was an earthquake, but they soon realized their new water tank had come crashing down. They thought it looked crooked, but their carpenter told them it was fine. Ethel commented, *"However, he was mistaken."* Gerald and Bernard were away for the night, having gone to a convivial where they were together with friends to eat, drink, and have a grand time at Cache Creek. It was noted that liquor was the primary provision for the gatherings, and many a drunken man and his money were flushed away as a result of this type of lifestyle. The only time they had alcohol at the house was on Christmas and holidays.

During a New Year's Eve party at the family home in Richmond, he concocted a punch of brandy, maraschino liqueur, sugar, grated nutmeg, sliced lemons, and an equal portion of boiling water. However, at least on one occasion, Gerald forgot to add the water.

Serves 1

1 teaspoon powdered sugar 3 dashes lemon juice 2 ounces gin 1 piece ice Seltzer water Lemon slice for garnish	1. Combine the sugar, lemon juice, and gin in a medium bar glass and stir. Add the ice, top with the seltzer water, and stir thoroughly.

SALADS, SOUPS & CONDIMENTS

PEA SOUP   39

VEGETABLE SOUP   40

CABBAGE SALAD WITH DRESSING   41

MR. BEAKBANE'S PICKLED FIGS   42

TOMATO KETCHUP   44

S.S. BRITANNIC

The S.S. *Britannic,* launched in 1874, was a luxury liner operated by the White Star Line and a proud member of the innovative *Oceanic*-class. Built to compete with Cunard's dominance on the transatlantic route, the *Britannic* showcased the era's cutting-edge maritime technology. Powered by a compound steam engine driving a single screw propeller and equipped with auxiliary sails, it balanced modernity with reliability. With a gross tonnage of 5,004 and plush first-class accommodations, the *Britannic* set new standards for comfort and style, catering to wealthy travelers and emigrants alike on the bustling Liverpool–New York route.

What truly distinguished the *Britannic* was its emphasis on luxury and passenger comfort over raw speed, reflecting the White Star Line's philosophy of "getting there in style." Its interiors featured elegant lounges, a smoking room for gentlemen, and spacious dining saloons. Even third-class passengers, often neglected on rival ships, were afforded decent accommodations, reflecting the company's forward-thinking approach. These features made the *Britannic* a favorite among travelers seeking a dependable and pleasant transatlantic crossing during the late 19th century.

During its service, the *Britannic* became synonymous with punctuality and reliability, enhancing the reputation of the White Star Line. Its design prioritized passenger comfort over speed, offering smooth transatlantic crossings in a time when sea travel was both adventurous and arduous. However, the rapid pace of maritime innovation soon rendered the *Britannic* obsolete. By the late 1890s, larger, faster, and more efficient ships eclipsed it, leading to its retirement after two decades of service. While its fame may have been overshadowed by later White Star vessels like the ill-fated R.M.S. *Titanic,* the *Britannic* played a vital role in establishing the company's prestige and setting a high bar for maritime luxury.

Contemporary illustration of S.S. Britannic, *ca. 1880.*

An artists' rendering from a reprint of the White Star Line Official Guide *(1877) of a Grand Saloon aboard a luxury liner like S.S.* Britannic.

Pea Soup

On April 20, 1885, while onboard the S.S. *Britannic* during her journey to America, Ethel donned one of her beautiful Victorian gowns. The boys all dressed in their tails and starched shirts and joined her as she celebrated her twenty-first birthday. They walked down the swaying ship's wooden corridors and then ascended the grand wooden staircase that was covered with an elegant carpet. They arrived at the *Britannic's* Grand Saloon dining hall where they settled into upholstered chairs. Ethel gazed at the long tables that were covered in crisp white linen and held fine China, polished silver, and expensive crystal glasses for wine and water. Pea soup was one of the menu items offered aboard the ship.

Serves 10

2 cups dried green split peas	1. Rinse peas with cold water and place them in a bowl, cover with water, and soak overnight. Drain and rinse.
Water for soaking	2. Place peas and ham bone in a Dutch oven. Add the 2 quarts of water and place on high heat.
2 quarts water for cooking	
1 meaty ham bone	3. Peel the onion, turnip, and carrot and cut them in half. Trim the celery ends and cut in half. Add the vegetables once the peas begin to boil. Add the salt and pepper and bring to a boil again.
1 large onion	
1 medium turnip	
1 large carrot	4. Reduce the heat to low and cover. Simmer for about 2 hours or until vegetables are tender.
3 celery stalks	5. Remove the ham bone and discard.
1 teaspoon salt	6. Run the soup through a sieve or use an immersion blender to blend until fairly smooth. Add a pinch of dried mint and serve with toasted bread.
1/2 teaspoon pepper	
Pinch dried mint	

SALADS, SOUPS & CONDIMENTS

Vegetable Soup

Their ranch meal schedule was quite precise, as was typical for many Victorians, and they breakfasted at seven, dined at noon, and ate supper at six. Ethel's first attempts at cooking were hit or miss at best, but she gained confidence as she practiced and found a recipe book. She also received recipe clippings and cookbooks from her family and Rowland Brown, from whom they lived with and eventually bought their California ranch land. One of her first dinners included vegetable soup, roast beef, potatoes, gravy, and a cream cake for dessert. She was quite proud at how easy she dealt with a cut of meat she had never seen but was disappointed when the lid from the pepper jar fell into the soup. When she penned letters home, she often described her cooking and the meals she prepared. It's not surprising because she never cooked before and seemed pleased with her ability to adapt and create tasty meals. She wrote this about her soup, *"Here we are at Mr. Brown's, and I have been housekeeping for two days now. We had a man to dinner to-day, so I was the only lady to six men. Perhaps you will be interested to know that we had vegetable soup, which was rather too peppery, as the lid of the pepper box fell off just at the critical moment."*

Serves 8

3 potatoes 2 turnips 1 carrot 1 onion 1 mushroom, any type 3 celery stalks 1 large slice bread 3 quarts water 1/2 teaspoon salt 1/4 teaspoon pepper	1. Peel the potatoes, turnips, carrot, and onion. Cut them and the remaining vegetables into small pieces. 2. Toast the bread until golden brown. Place the vegetables and bread into a large stock pot and add the water, salt, and pepper. Simmer gently for about 1 to 2 hours until the vegetables are soft and reduced to a thick pulp. 3. Run the mixture through a sieve or use an immersion blender to puree. Season to taste and serve.

Cabbage Salad with Dressing

Ethel's neighbors often gifted her with an ample supply of fresh vegetables because they knew she was in need as her husband and his brothers tried to get their ranch prospering. She had no choice but to experiment with various recipes. One day she created her own version of coleslaw, which the men thoroughly enjoyed. She wrote this about it. *"We only have one cow here, and she is nearly dry, so we are always being left destitute of butter, as we do not get enough in from town to last very long, and then have to content ourselves with treacle (a dark syrup). It is so difficult to know what to cook when one has neither butter nor milk not suet. You would have been amused at my salad yesterday. I had a quarter of a cabbage left (they are so enormous that they will not get into any saucepan whole), so I chopped it up small and made a dressing of eggs, mustard, salt and milk; there was neither oil nor vinegar. The boys ate it all up and said what a good salad it was."*

Serves 6

3 cups shredded cabbage 2 egg yolks 1/2 teaspoon salt 1/2 teaspoon dry mustard 1/2 cup milk 1 tablespoon shredded carrots	1. Combine the eggs, salt, and mustard in a small bowl and beat until smooth. Set aside. 2. Put the milk in a sauce pan over medium heat and scald the milk until there are bubbles on the outside of the pan. Remove from heat. 3. To temper the eggs, add about a tablespoon of hot milk to the bowl with the egg mixture, stir quickly. Add this mixture to the hot milk and stir. Place the pan back on medium heat and stir constantly until the mixture just begins to thicken or coat a spoon. Remove from heat and pour over the shredded cabbage. Top with the carrots. Chill for about 2 or 3 hours. Stir before serving.

Mrs. Beakbane's Pickled Figs

Thomas and Margaret Beakbane were Ethel's closest English neighbors when she lived in Lake County, California. Despite having good neighbors like the Beakbanes, everyone was spread apart, and that made Ethel feel isolated. Margaret had rescued a little lamb and knew of Ethel's loneliness and affection for animals. It didn't take much convincing from Margaret for Ethel to adopt her. As Margaret suspected, Ethel fell in love with her new little lamb and named it Bimbi, after Ouida's stories. Bimbi is a collection of children's stories from Italy and Tyrol. Ouida was the pen name of the English novelist Louise de la Rame and comes from her mispronunciation of her first name as a young child. She was also an animal rights activist and an animal rescuer and at times owned as many as thirty dogs. She was a woman after Ethel's own heart. Bimbi quickly took to Ethel and she to Bimbi and even sat on her lap like a cat. After a week, Bimbi became so attached to Ethel that she followed her around the house and bleated loudly if she couldn't find her. She wrote home about her new pet. *"Bimbi is getting so fat and fond of me, that she won't leave me for a minute and bleats in a most piteous way if she cannot find me. She lets me wash her and is quite a companion to me."*

After the Hertslets left Lake County, Thomas went on to do many things in the area. In 1900, he was still farming in the Lower Lake area with his wife and their two daughters, Margaret and Manzanita. By April 1910, he had given up on farming and was back to the real estate business that he and Gerald had once partnered in. Beakbane Island is named after Thomas and is in Clear Lake. Margaret took advantage of the white figs that grew in the area and made these pickled figs.

The Beakbane Ranch ca. 1885

Makes About 7 Quarts

7 pounds white figs 4 pounds white sugar 1 pint white vinegar 1 ounce cinnamon 1 ounce cloves	1. Wash figs thoroughly in clean water. Cover figs with water and boil for 2 minutes. Drain. 2. Place the figs in a large pot and alternate with layers of sugar. Heat over medium low heat and bring slowly to a boil. Add vinegar and spices and boil for 30 minutes. Remove the fruit with a perforated skimmer and spread upon dishes to cool. 3. Boil remaining syrup until thick. Pack fruit in jars and pour in the boiling syrup, leaving 1/2-inch headspace. Adjust lids and process 50 minutes in a water bath. Allow to cool and check seals.

Tomato Ketchup

Ethel's cooking skills improved, and she shared her stories with her family. In 1885, she wrote, *"I am writing in the kitchen, to keep an eye on a huge thing of tomato-ketchup, which is boiling on the stove. The tomatoes cost two shillings a box, one by a half foot and one foot deep. Not dear, were they? If our English servants once felt the comfort of these American stoves, they would never put up with our ranges. It is so much handier having it low so that one can stir things easily, and in hot weather it is a comfort to have the fire all shut it."*

Makes About 2 Pints

2 quarts tomatoes (or about 4 pounds.) 1 cup apple cider vinegar 2 tablespoons pickling salt 2 teaspoons red pepper flakes 1 tablespoon black pepper 1 tablespoon allspice 1 tablespoon cloves 2 tablespoons ground mustard	1. Blanch the tomatoes and remove their skin. Place everything into a blender and puree (or use an immersion blender). Then place into a large stock pot and gently boil for about 4 hours or until thickened. 2. Place cooled mixture in bottles and refrigerate. This can also be preserved by pouring the ketchup into hot, sterilized jars (leaving 1/2-inch headspace) and cooking in a hot water bath for 15 minutes.

VEGETABLES & SIDE DISHES

ASPARAGUS 47

PEAS 48

BOILED PARSNIPS 49

SAGE & ONION STUFFING 52 49

MASHED POTATOES 50

BROWNED POTATOES 51

BAKED SWEET POTATOES 51

APPLESAUCE 52

BOILED BEETS 52

FRENCH BEANS, BOILED 53

GLAZED CARROTS 54

CUCUMBERS, DRESSED 55

SUMMER SQUASH 56

BAKED TOMATOES 56

LIMA BEANS 57

MACARONI NEAPOLITAINE 59

MASHED TURNIPS 59

TOMATO SAUCE 59

LETTUCE & TOMATO SALAD
  WITH FRENCH DRESSING 60

THE PALACE HOTEL

The Palace Hotel as it looked when Ethel stayed there in the 1880s.

Asparagus

Despite feeling comfortable at the Palace Hotel in San Francisco upon their arrival in California, they knew they couldn't afford to stay there any longer. So, on May 8, 1885, they checked out and found cheaper, but respectable, accommodations for Ethel, Bernard, and Henry at the Stockton Street House near Chinatown. Gerald and Louis were leaving for Lake County to see if they could find some homesteading land. Ethel settled into her rooming house at 218 Stockton where she had a small, but clean room that included breakfast. While she appreciated the breakfast, she was not happy that she had to leave the Stockton for her midday and evening meals. She managed to find one dinner for twenty cents that included a huge plate of roast beef, potatoes, asparagus, a cup of coffee, and as much bread and butter as she could eat. She got spoiled at the Palace with the strawberries and cream, so she ordered a large plate of them for ten cents. Slowly, Ethel began dealing with her day-to-day responsibilities. Three weeks' worth of laundry needed cleaning, and she set out to find a source. She was shocked at what the Chinese laundries charged, which was ten cents per item, except for handkerchiefs. Their room at the Stockton only cost fifty cents per day! She was also annoyed that the servants in the homes refused to clean boots, so the boys had to go out and find a street vendor to do the job.

Serves 2-4

1 pound asparagus 1/4 cup oil 2 tablespoons white vinegar Salt and pepper, to taste	1. Snap the ends off the asparagus and cook in salted boiling water until tender, which should take about 15 minutes depending upon the thickness. 2. Combine the remaining ingredients together and whisk until blended. 3. Place cooked asparagus onto a cutting board and cut into pieces and place into a bowl. Pour the oil and vinegar over the asparagus, season to taste, and serve.

Peas

During their ocean journey to America in 1885, the S.S. *Britannic's* dinner menu, which was the midday meal, was the largest and included veal cutlets a la Zingara, curried duck and green peas, rabbit and bacon, and ribs of beef and potatoes. For dessert, Ethel could choose from Stilton, Wiltshire, and Cheshire cheeses.

Serves 4

2 1/2 cups fresh peas 1/2 teaspoon sugar 1 teaspoon salt 2 tablespoons butter Salt and pepper, to taste	1. Place peas, sugar, and salt into a sauce pan of boiling water and cook over medium high heat for about 20 minutes or until the peas are tender. Remove from the heat and strain. Place back into the pan and add the butter and season with salt and pepper.

Landing Stage, Liverpool, England, ca. 1885

Boiled Parsnips

This is one of the many dishes that Ethel and the boys would have enjoyed on their journey to America aboard the S.S *Britannic* when they sailed to America for the first time. Parsnips were a popular vegetable during Ethel's lifetime.

Serves 4-6

1 tablespoon extra-virgin olive oil 1 tablespoon unsalted butter 2 pounds parsnips, peeled and sliced into circles 1 cup water Salt and pepper, to taste	1. Put the olive oil and butter into a large pot over medium-high heat. Add the vegetables and toss to coat them. 2. Add water, a 1/2 teaspoon of salt, and bring to a boil, then reduce to a simmer. Cover the pot and cook until the parsnips are tender, about 20 minutes. Drain if any water is left. Add additional butter if desired and salt and pepper to taste.

Sage and Onion Stuffing

While Ethel didn't specify how she used her onions, this recipe appeared in one of her favorite recipe books. This stuffing was used for goose, duck, and pork.

Makes 2-3 Cups

4 large onions 10 fresh sage leaves 1 cup bread crumbs 3 tablespoons butter, melted 1 egg Salt and pepper, to taste	1. Peel the onions and place them into a pan of salted boiling water. After 2 minutes, add the sage leaves and boil for another 3 minutes. Remove from the heat and drain. When cool enough to handle, chop both finely. 2. Place into a bowl and add the bread crumbs, butter, eggs, and salt and pepper. 3. Allow to cool before stuffing.

Mashed Potatoes

As the days went on at the ranch in Lake County, Ethel became busier, and even though the boys did help, she still felt weary. For two days they washed six-dozen handkerchiefs, one dozen shirts, and a multitude of other garments. Add to that making bread, which needed to rise overnight, preparing breakfast, cleaning up, preparing the noon-day dinner, and shelling peas and peeling potatoes, she was exhausted. After dinner, she pulled out the washboard, soap, and wash tub and continued washing until three thirty. Ethel took a much needed, albeit short, break and then swept out the sitting room. She then put the kettle on to boil, pulled down the cups and saucers, and dumped the loose-leaf tea into the pot to steep. Her laundry chores were done for the day, but the next day all that clean laundry had to be ironed. She stoked up the stove and placed the heavy iron on it to heat up. She then tackled the mound of clean, wrinkled laundry as she pushed the hot, three-pound cast iron until her back ached.

Serves 4

- 2 pounds potatoes, peeled
- 1 tablespoon salt for boiling the potatoes
- 1 cup broth or milk
- 4 tablespoons butter
- Salt and pepper, to taste

1. Fill a pot with water and add the tablespoon salt. Bring to a boil over high heat. While the water is coming to a boil, slice the potatoes into 1/2-inch slices and place in the water. Cook until the potatoes are soft. Drain well and return to the pot. Cook over medium heat to absorb any excess water. Mash the potatoes and then add the broth, butter, and salt and pepper.

Browned Potatoes

Ethel's first trip into Lower Lake occurred in mid-1885 when she and her Burns Valley neighbor, Miss May Mitchel, hitched up Piper the horse to her wagon and drove to the town to pick up her mail. Lower Lake was less than impressive to her with its one broad street, a hotel, a tiny Roman Catholic Church, a Methodist one, and a few houses scattered about. Ethel wrote home about Lower Lake. *"You would be amused at what they call 'town.'"* Already disappointed with the town, she became frustrated with the stores because they sold a variety of everything, and the items were *"all mixed up and in confusing places."* They then paid a visit to their local farmer's market, where they found Peter de Lucci, the green grocer.

Serves 4-6

10 to 12 small new potatoes, scrubbed 1/4 cup butter, melted 1/2 teaspoon salt 1/4 teaspoon freshly ground pepper	1. Place the potatoes in cold water and place over high heat. Bring to a boil and then drain and pat dry. Place the butter into a frying pan over medium high heat, and when melted, add the potatoes. 2. Cook the potatoes for about 20 minutes or until browned. Season with salt and pepper.

Baked Sweet Potatoes

While Ethel wouldn't enjoy this dish until much later in her life, when she traveled on the R.M.S. *Etruria*. See the ice cream entry on page 99 for the story behind this recipe.

Serves 4

2 large sweet potatoes, peeled and sliced 1/2 cup granulated sugar 2 tablespoons butter, cubed	1. Place sweet potatoes into a pot of boiling, lightly salted water and cook until tender, about 20-30 minutes. Drain and set aside. 2. Butter a baking dish and add a layer of potatoes and sprinkle with sugar. Add another layer of potatoes and sugar and continue this until the potatoes are used up. Top with additional sugar if necessary. Dot the top with the butter. 3. Cover and bake at 350°F for about 20 minutes and then uncover and bake an additional 20 minutes.

Applesauce

See the Loin of Pork recipe for more details on this entry. This applesauce is served with that dish.

Serves 8

3 pounds apples (about 6 medium) 1/3 cup water 2 to 3 tablespoons sugar or to taste 1 tablespoon butter	1. Peel, core, and chop the apples. Place them in a large sauce pan and add the water. Boil until the apples are soft. Add the sugar and butter and beat well with a masher or mixer.

Boiled Beets

Ethel was fortunate to live in Lake County, California, where fresh vegetables were abundant. She wrote back to England in the summer of 1885. *"We have plenty of vegetables, and I experiment upon them! Beet-root is very good hot!"*

Serves 4-6

4 medium beets, stems and roots removed Water 1/2 teaspoon salt 2 to 3 tablespoons butter Salt and pepper, to taste	1. Bring a large pot of water to a boil and add the salt. Place beets into boiling water and cook for about 20 minutes or until tender. Remove from heat and drain. Peel the beets when they are cool enough to handle. They can be put into an ice water bath to speed up the process. 2. Cut them into thick slices and return to the pan. Add the butter and season to taste.

French Beans, Boiled

On another trip to Peter de Lucchi's store in town, Ethel discussed the cost of goods. *"My green grocer, Peter de Lucchi, is such a pleasant little fellow, an Italian. To give you an idea of prices, I will tell you what we bought this morning of him for four bits. Two vegetable marrows (summer squashes they call them), half a large bucketful of French beans, a dozen beet-roots, a dozen turnips, and five enormous onions."* This photo shows the town of Lower Lake in 1888 where Ethel shopped at Peter De Lucchi's store.

Serves 4

4 cups fresh green beans Water 1 teaspoon salt Pinch of baking soda 1 tablespoon butter Salt and pepper, to taste	1. Trim the beans to remove ends and if needed, remove strings. Cut the beans into 4 to 6 pieces on a slant. Fill a large pot with water and bring it to a boil with the salt and baking soda. Add the green beans and cook for about 20 minutes or until tender. Remove from the heat, drain, and return to the pot. Add the butter and salt and pepper.

The town of Lower Lake, California, ca. 1888.

VEGETABLES & SIDE DISHES • 53

Glazed Carrots

Ethel and her English community in Lake County, California, often sought relief from the oppressive heat at the local lakes. It was on one of those hot June days in 1885 when she called upon Miss May to accompany her to one of their favorite lakes. They hitched up a wagon and headed out. After languishing in the cool water and feeling refreshed, Ethel took Miss May home. Upon their arrival, her friend Effie Keatinge greeted Ethel and gave her a bounty of carrots, turnips, and onions. After a proper visit and some tea, Ethel departed. She placed her hat on her head like a proper Victorian lady but felt "scandalous and common" as she walked home with the sack slung over her back with her long hair freely blowing in the breeze. She even wrote home about it. *"You would have been astonished if you could have seen me trudging up the hill with my hair flying about loose in the wind, a huge hat on, and a sack on my back."* The walk home defeated the whole point of cooling off, and she was once again hot. Despite being unrefreshed, Ethel had duties that needed attention. It was time for tea, so she chopped firewood since the boys were in town, lit the stove, and set about preparing the afternoon ritual.

Serves 2-4

2 tablespoons salt 6 to 8 carrots, peeled and cut as you like 1 cup stock 1 teaspoon fine sugar 2 tablespoons butter	1. Place a saucepan of water over high heat and bring to a boil. Add 1 tablespoon salt and add the carrots and boil for about 20 minutes or until tender. Drain and dry with a cloth or paper towels. 2. Place them in a frying pan and add enough stock just to cover. Add the butter, sugar, and 1 tablespoon salt and bring to a boil. Reduce the heat to simmer and cook until the liquid evaporates and the carrots become glazed.

The Burnes Valley Cricket Club, ca. 1887.

Cucumbers, Dressed

Cricket was very popular in Burns Valley because of all its British immigrants. It was so popular that Charles Owens, one of the area's first investors, formed the Burns Valley Cricket Club in 1887. He was a Lancashire, England, cricketer who knew the local British cricketers would flock to a club pavilion and cricket field. Owens was also Ethel and Gerald's neighbor. Gerald's friend and business partner, Thomas Beakbane, became the captain of the cricket club. According to Henry Mauldin's history of Lake County, *"When the Englishmen came, they brought with them the desire to continue a sport which they indulged in England—the playing of cricket. A place was set up near the present Garner Resort, and it became a popular sport for the County."* The men played inter-squad games with the smokers against the non-smokers. The gentlemen appeared in white linen coats, buttoned to the neck, much like those who dressed for dinner in India. Ethel often entertained her fellow British neighbors, and at one meal, in addition to mutton as the main course, she served dishes made with fresh tomatoes and cucumbers.

Serves 4

2 large cucumbers Salt and pepper, to taste 3 tablespoons oil 4 tablespoons vinegar	1. Slice the cucumbers very thinly with a knife or mandolin. Place them on a serving platter and season with salt and pepper. Drizzle the oil and vinegar over the cucumbers and serve.

VEGETABLES & SIDE DISHES • 55

Summer Squash

Another one of the vegetables that Ethel experimented on was squash—either zucchini or yellow.

Serves 4

2 large zucchinis Salt and pepper, to taste 2 tablespoons butter or to taste	1. Add water and a little salt to a large pot of water and bring to a boil. Peel and remove the seeds from the zucchini and cut into pieces. Add the pieces to the boiling water and cook until tender or about 40 minutes. When done, drain and return to the pot. 2. Add the butter and whip into a creamy pulp. Add salt and pepper to taste.

Baked Tomatoes

While tomatoes were expensive, Ethel served them occasionally for her dinner parties. Mrs. Beeton's cookery book noted this recipe paired well with roasted meat.

Serves 4-6

8 or 10 tomatoes, sliced thick Salt and pepper, to taste 4 tablespoons butter Breadcrumbs 1/4 cup clarified butter	1. Layer the tomato slices in a deep baking dish and season with salt and pepper. Add the butter between the layers. Add enough breadcrumbs to cover the tomatoes and drizzle with the clarified butter. Bake at 350°F for about 20 to 30 minutes or until golden.

Lima Beans

This is one of the vegetables Ethel prepared when she and Claude first arrived in New York and were struggling in the 1890s. They grew fond of lima beans and valued their nutritional value. For additional story details, see the currant loaf recipe.

Serves 4-6

16 ounces frozen baby lima beans	1. Cook the lima beans in boiling, salted water as directed on the package.
1/2 cup heavy whipping cream	2. Drain the beans well and add the cream and butter.
2 tablespoons butter	3. Taste and add salt and pepper as desired.
Salt, to taste	
Freshly ground black pepper, to taste	

Ethel with her cousin and future husband Claude Barry in the 1890s.

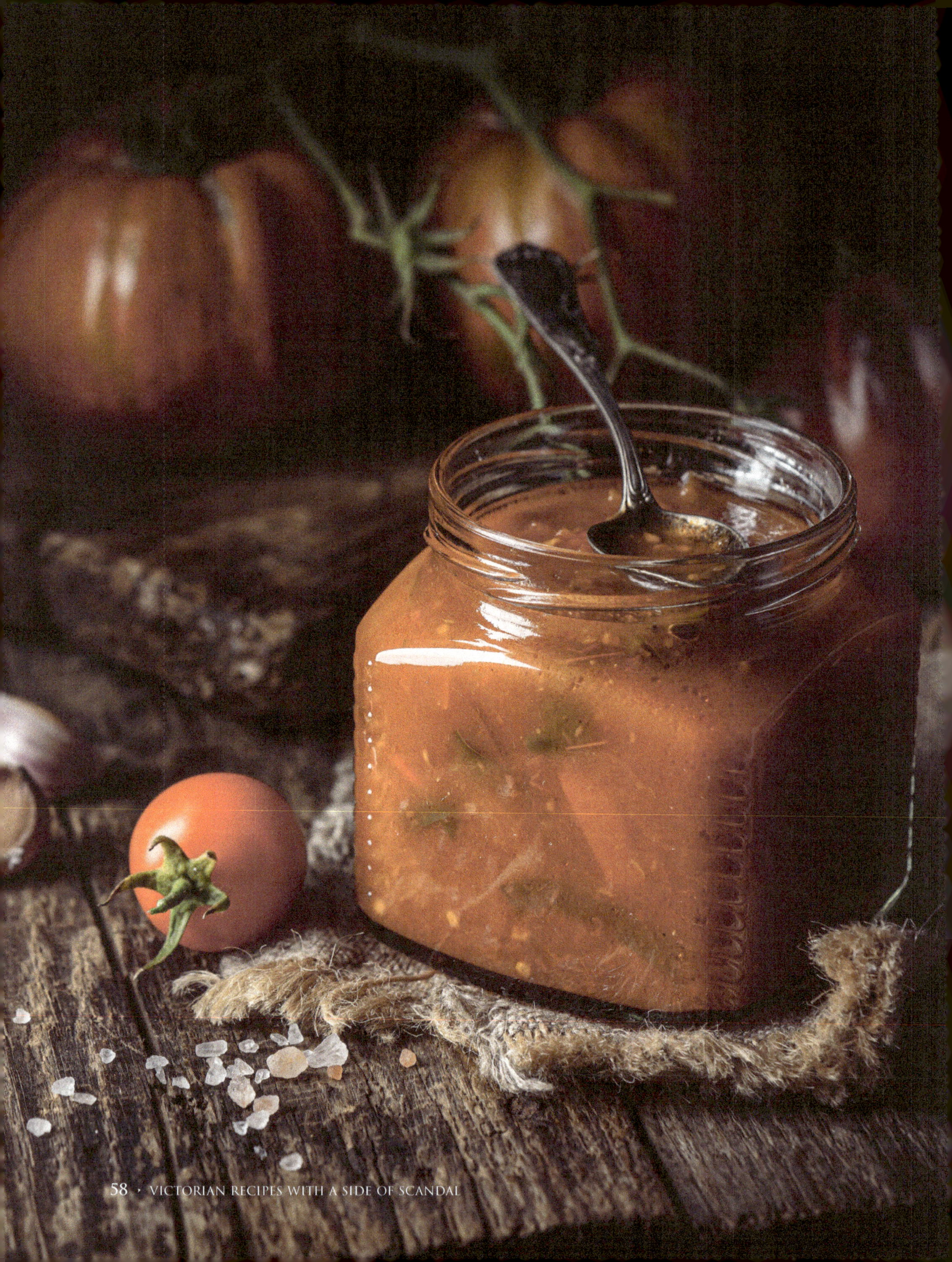

Macaroni Neapolitan

This recipe was also called "Macaroni Italienne" or "Macaroni Italian-Style." During her time, the most common macaroni noodle available in the U.S. was spaghetti but was referred to as macaroni. Some recipes call for it to be cooked and then cut into pieces, while others suggested breaking it dry before boiling. See the ice cream entry on page 99 for the story behind this recipe.

Serves 2-4

3/4 cup macaroni noodle of your choice, uncooked 1/2 onion, peeled and cut in half 2 teaspoons butter 1 1/2 cups tomato sauce 1/2 cup grated Parmesan cheese 1 tablespoon red wine	1. Place the macaroni, onion, and butter in a medium pot of boiling water. Cook until the macaroni is barely tender, about 15 minutes. Drain and return the macaroni to the pot. Add the tomato sauce, cheese, and wine; heat through and serve.

Mashed Turnips

Serves 4-6

6 large turnips, peeled and chopped 1 1/2 teaspoons salt 2 tablespoons butter Cayenne or white pepper to taste Cream or milk, optional	1. Place the turnips in enough boiling water to cover them and add the salt. Boil over high heat until tender. Remove from heat and drain. 2. Put the turnips back in the pan and mash. Add the butter and pepper and stir over low heat until the butter has melted. A little cream or milk can also be added.

Tomato Sauce

Makes 1 1/2 cups

1 3/4 cups crushed tomatoes 1/4 cup chopped onion 2 teaspoons butter 2 tablespoons flour 1/4 teaspoon salt 1/2 teaspoon freshly ground pepper 1/2 teaspoon oregano 1/2 teaspoon chopped fresh parsley	1. In a large skillet, cook the tomatoes and onion over medium heat until onions are lightly browned. Strain and set aside. 2. Add the butter and flour to the skillet and cook over medium heat for 2 to 3 minutes. Gradually stir in the tomatoes, onion, and oregano; cook until slightly thickened. Add the parsley before serving.

Lettuce and Tomato Salad with French Dressing

This is one of the many dishes onboard the R.M.S. *Etruria*. See the ice cream entry on page 99 for the story behind this recipe.

Serves 4-6

- 2 or 3 types of lettuces, Romaine, endive, etc.
- Salt and pepper, to taste
- 1 cup chopped tomatoes
- 1/2 teaspoon chopped chives
- 2 tablespoons combined of chervil parsley and tarragon
- 3 tablespoons oil, any will do
- 1 tablespoon white or champagne vinegar
- 1 teaspoon French mustard

1. Wash and dry the lettuces and then tear or chop into bite-size pieces. Place into a mixing bowl and season with salt and pepper. Add the tomatoes and herbs and gently toss to blend.
2. Mix the oil, vinegar, and mustard in a small bowl and blend until well combined. Pour over the lettuces and toss just before serving.

Contemporary illustration of a salad similar to the one served aboard R.M.S. Etruria.

MAIN MEALS

WHOLE FRIED TROUT 63

PAN FRIED TROUT 64

SALMON CUTLETS WITH
CAPER SAUCE 66

SALMON CAKES 67

ROAST CHICKEN 68

ROAST TURKEY WITH
BACON LEMON DRESSING 70

LOIN OF PORK WITH
APPLESAUCE 71

TOAD IN A HOLE 72

ROAST BEEF WITH GRAVY 75

FRIED STEAK & ONIONS 75

CHILI CON CARNE 76

MUTTON STEW 78

MUTTON CUTLETS 79

DRESSED CRAB 80

PICKLED OYSTERS 80

ETHEL EXPERIENCES THE CHINESE IN SAN FRANCISCO

Before Ethel headed to San Rafael she lunched with the wife of Mr. D. from the S.S. *Britannic*, who had a home in the city. Mrs. D. took Ethel to Chinatown for lunch. From what Ethel could see everything seemed rather respectable, but Mrs. D. advised her that was not the case below ground. She told Ethel about a time when she was escorted by police officers three stories below Chinatown. She witnessed people living in tombs in utter filth and told Ethel she had never seen such horrors.

Despite that, everything above ground proved interesting for Ethel. After lunch the two women ventured into various Chinese shops and visited the Joss House. It was in this Chinese temple where immigrants worshipped a variety of indigenous Chinese deities, saints, and supernatural beings. They were especially popular in western frontier towns that had Chinatowns, like San Francisco and Deadwood, South Dakota.

Ethel was quite impressed with its gold carvings, incense burning, and the arranged peacock feathers. However, not all sat well with a very Christian Ethel who remarked, *"…they pray to a repulsive idol."*

This is what the San Francisco area looked like when Ethel visited it and saw the Joss House, ca. 1880s.

The *San Francisco Bulletin* ran a large story about the Chinese living in the city. They reported that over thirteen thousand Chinese men were living in Chinatown, and surprisingly, only twenty-two-hundred of them were employed in the manufacturing industry in the city, including cigar making, boot and shoe making, clothing and underwear makers, and other miscellaneous trades. The other eleven thousand were both skilled and unskilled and working outside the city limits. An additional two thousand Chinese immigrants included women, children, and prostitutes. Of them, some three hundred and seventy were prostitutes.

Whole Fried Trout

Ethel spent some time with George and Mrs. Stanley at their San Rafael bungalow in May 1885 before they found their land. She arrived at the Stanleys' small wooden home that was plainly decorated. The structure was basic, but comfortable, and Ethel thought it was paradise. The wrap-around veranda was covered with honeysuckle and exuded an aromatic fragrance that perfumed open windows of the house. Hummingbirds, with their ruby throats and shimmering green backs, enjoyed them, too, as they dipped their tiny beaks into the flowers and chirped in excitement. Ethel felt sincerely happy at this place and wrote home. *"I so wish you could be here to see it, you would revel in it; and the air, too, is so light and refreshing, just like Switzerland."*

George took Ethel out to see the countryside on May 15, 1885. The dirt roads were steep, rocky, and filled with ruts, so she had to hold on tightly as the wagon bounced over them. They finally reached a small lake in a valley that was surrounded by wooded hills where Mr. Stanley fished. As he waited for nibbles on his line, Ethel watched exquisite red and bright blue dragonflies dance on the lake. He caught about eight or nine trout and in true fisherman form told her if it hadn't been so windy, he would have caught more. Happily, for Ethel, Mr. Stanley chose a better road to take them home. This time, they navigated a ridge on top of the hill, which afforded beautiful views of the lush valleys and clear streams.

Serves 2-4

1 pound whole fresh trout, cleaned
2 tablespoons flour
1/2 teaspoon salt
2 tablespoons butter
Lemon wedges, optional
Fresh parsley, chopped, optional

1. Combine the flour with salt in a pie pan or dish. Lay the fish in the flour and coat on both sides.
2. Melt the butter in a large frying pan over medium-high heat. Gently place fish in the pan and fry for approximately 4 to 5 minutes per side or until golden brown. Allow the fish to rest for about 10 minutes before cutting. Garnish with a wedge of lemon and parsley if desired.

Pan-Fried Trout

Ethel saw many sites when they traversed America and the prairies as they made their way to California in 1885. She was appalled at the "hideous yellow desert" she saw as the train entered the Green River area in Wyoming Territory. Four hundred people lived in the town that began as a "hell on wheels" makeshift tent city that once supported the workers along the Union Pacific line. Some twenty years later, after the railroad workers moved, passengers lined the wooden platform waiting on the arrival of the train. Many craned their necks in anticipation of the morning train as it steamed into the small, wooden-framed station. The train stopped, and the passengers disembarked as they made their way to breakfast at the Green River Eating House in the Desert House. Ethel walked onto the platform and gazed at the red rock towers just beyond the Desert House that sat right next door to the train depot. They entered the white building through tall Victorian-glass paned doors and sat down to eat. After they finished breakfast at the Green River Eating House in the Desert House in Green River, Wyoming Territory, they boarded the train and five stops later pulled into Evanston, Wyoming Territory. Chinamen, whose hands were thrust under the loose folds of their dark-blue blouses, *"shuffled up and down the platform on their cork soled shoes as their long pigtails swayed halfway down to their heels."*

As the train pulled into the station, Ethel heard the call, "twenty minutes for dinner." This stop was a treat for them, and they raced to the Mountain Trout House, which was known for its delicious trout. It was opened by C.W., W.T., and J.B. Kitchen, who also operated the Desert House in Green River and several other hotels and restaurants at various train stations. As she approached, Ethel gazed at a large dish of fresh trout sitting atop ice in one of the front windows. When she entered the hotel, she saw a good deal of Chinese and Japanese pictures, some stuffed heads of Buffalo, and that of lesser game. Years earlier *Leslie's Weekly* wrote about it. *"In the little hotel, a gem in its way of neatness and order, we find the dining room given over to their (the Chinamen's) presiding influence, and nothing can be more soothing to the traveler's nerves than such a silent, soft-stepping, light-handed attendant, gliding behind one's chair like a shadow, always smiling and deferential."*

The Chinese influence was seen in Evanston because they had a little Chinatown north of the tracks, where a cluster of dirty, unpainted shanties were crowded together. Their only adornment was long strips of red paper around the door posts. By the time Ethel arrived, American sentiment had changed, and the Anti-Chinese Movement was gaining popularity. Businesses were often blackballed if they hired Chinese workers. Ethel noticed this attitude since the English had no problem with them. She penned, *"We have come to the land of Chinamen servants, and it is extraordinary what an aversion the Americans have to them; they will hardly go to a restaurant where they are served by them."*

With satisfied appetites, they boarded the train again and steamed into a region of snowy mountains, steep canyons, and raging rivers. Ethel's mood changed with the terrain, and she found herself enjoying the beautiful scenery.

Panoramic illustration of Green River, Wyoming Territory in 1875.

Serves 2-4

1 cup breadcrumbs or flour 1/2 teaspoon salt 1/4 teaspoon ground pepper 2 tablespoons butter for frying 2 tablespoons oil 1 pound trout fillets, 1-inch thick Parsley or watercress for garnish	1. Mix the crumbs and salt and pepper in a bowl and set aside. 2. Melt the butter and oil over medium high heat in a large frying pan. 3. Coat the fillets in the crumbs and fry until golden on each side or about 2 to 3 mins. Turn and cook for an additional 2 mins. The fish should flake when done. 4. Remove from the pan and garnish with parsley.

Salmon Cutlets with Caper Sauce

Even though Ethel had blossomed as a cook during her time in Lake County, she grew frustrated with her menu. In addition to her cooking issues, shopping was another chore, and when she needed supplies, she had to take a rugged wagon ride to Lower Lake. While she relied upon tinned meat and salmon, which they enjoyed, she knew this was too expensive to dine on all the time. She cooked a lot of bacon for the men, but she detested it. She wrote home, *"I am really at my wits end to know what to provide to eat. The tinned meat and salmon is very good but too expensive to eat always, and bacon has palled upon all of us."*

Serves 4

4 (6-ounce) salmon fillets 1/2 teaspoon salt 1/2 teaspoon freshly ground black pepper 6 tablespoons butter 1 tablespoon lemon juice or caper liquid 3 tablespoons capers, drained	1. Season the fillets with salt and pepper. Heat a large skillet over medium high heat and add 3 tablespoons of butter. Once melted, add the salmon fillets skin side up and cook for 2 to 3 minutes until cooked about halfway to center of the thick part of salmon. Reduce to medium heat and flip the salmon. Cook for 5 minutes. 2. While the salmon is cooking, melt the remaining butter in a small saucepan over low heat and add the capers and lemon juice. Stir to blend and keep warm. 3. Once the salmon is cooked, pour the sauce over salmon, and serve. The internal temperature should be between 125°F to 130°F in the center when removed.

Salmon Cakes

While living on their ranch in Lake County, Ethel hosted a dinner for seven local bachelors. She once again pulled out her cookbooks and flipped through them to choose her menu. She wrote, *"First, salmon cakes—it is the only fish I can get that is nice and dainty."*

Serves 4-8

3 teaspoons butter 15 ounces canned salmon, drained, or 1 1/2 cups cooked salmon 1 small onion, finely chopped 1/2 teaspoon freshly ground pepper 1/2 teaspoon salt 1 tablespoon chopped fresh thyme 1 tablespoon chopped fresh marjoram 1 cup fresh breadcrumbs 1 cup mashed potatoes 1 egg white, lightly beaten Lemon and parsley for garnish	1. Heat 1 1/2 teaspoons of butter in a large nonstick skillet over medium-high heat. Add onion, salt and pepper, and herbs and cook until softened, or about 3 minutes. Remove from the heat. 2. Place the salmon in a medium bowl and flake apart with a fork, being sure to remove any bones and skin. Add the onion mixture, breadcrumbs, potatoes, and mix well. Shape into 8 patties. 3. Heat the remaining 1 1/2 teaspoons of butter in the pan over medium heat. Add 4 patties and cook until the undersides are golden, 2 to 3 minutes. Gently flip and cook for an additional 2 to 3 minutes. Keep them warm on a baking sheet while finishing the other patties. Bake the salmon cakes at 350°F until golden on top and heated through for about 15 to 20 minutes.

Roast Chicken

While at her ranch, Ethel planned a supper for some guests, but on the day of her meal, Adamson, the mutton man, came to her house and, much to her angst, advised he couldn't catch his sheep. She had to come up with another protein option because Lower Lake was too far to go with the meal just hours away. It wouldn't have bothered her if it were just her and the boys since they often had meatless meals, but Ethel was not about to have a dinner party without meat. She asked Gerald to get her some chickens from their coop, so he killed an old rooster and a young chicken. With a slight meal change, Ethel donned her cooking apron and got to work. She was quite pleased with her efforts, and her guests were as well. She noted, *"The dish presented a most extraordinary appearance, one bird being as large as a small turkey and the other the size of a pigeon. They were very good indeed. The chickens were an awful extravagance."* Ethel, the once well-attended-to socialite, was successfully settling into her domestic duties. She often wrote home about her cooking challenges, and this meal was one of them. She penned, *"I seem to be always writing about food and cooking; but you understand what an interesting subject it is to me just now from its novelty…."*

Serves anywhere from 4-8 (depending upon the size of the chicken)

1 whole chicken, about 4 pounds 4 tablespoons butter, softened Salt and freshly ground black pepper, to taste 4 tablespoons flour 2 tablespoons butter	1. Preheat oven to 450°F. 2. Remove neck and giblets from inside the cavity of the chicken and pat dry all over with paper towels. Rub the butter over the chicken and salt and pepper. 3. Roast the chicken, uncovered, at 450°F for 15 minutes and then reduce the oven to 350°F. Roast 20 minutes per pound or until internal temperature (inserted on middle of thigh and breast) reaches 165°F. The skin should be golden brown, and the juices should run clear. About 20 minutes before the chicken should be done, sprinkle it with flour and then ladle the pan juices over it. Do this two or three times before it's done to make a thin pan gravy. 4. Remove chicken from the oven and cover with foil so it can rest for 10 minutes before carving.

GERALD'S INABILITY

A California paper wrote this about the Hertslets' chickens and poultry venture, *"Hatching under duress is extremely wearing on the most robust hen… most of their feathers had fallen out, their spirits were broken, and it is said that a more disreputable appearing colony of hens was never seen in Lake County. They nearly all died off, and the chicks were destroyed by rats and skunks."* The Hertslet brothers had gained a reputation in the valley for not finishing their projects, and this one was no different. Even Gerald's family recalled, *"Gerald was a handsome, engaging man, but the ability to concentrate on one career eluded him."*

He also left Ethel alone on a regular basis to go hang out with his friends. On June 13, 1885 Ethel wrote, *"We had such a scare last night. Our water tank fell down, and it will cost a great deal to rebuild it. It has looked crooked for some time, but the carpenter thought it was quite safe. However, he was mistaken. Gerald and Bernard were both out for the night, having gone to a 'convivial' at Cache Creek, and about 4 a.m.. came an appalling crash, and we all rushed to the veranda in our night gear--thinking an earthquake had happened. We soon found out what it was."*

Cache Creek, ca. 1880s.

Roast Turkey with Bacon Lemon Dressing

About a week before Christmas in 1885, Gerald made his way to the yard to procure some turkeys. They needed to be plucked, but they had no idea how to do it. So, Ethel pulled down Mrs. Beeton's cookery book, and they referred to it "every two minutes" for step by step instructions. Despite having to pluck the turkey, Ethel seemed fairly happy about her first Christmas as a rancher's wife and became very excited about making her first Christmas Day dinner. She was concerned when she went to prep the turkeys because they smelled so bad, but she needed them and took the risk. To her delight, they came out just fine. Their neighbor, Mr. Scranton, picked them up in his wagon, and they spent Christmas Eve with him. They were supposed to walk back but ended up spending the night because the rain-soaked roads were too treacherous for a five-month pregnant Ethel to walk back.

Serves 6 (10-pound bird)

10-15 pound turkey Salt and pepper, to taste 4 tablespoons flour 2 tablespoons butter *Dressing for Turkey* 2 ounces bacon, diced 8 tablespoons butter Rind of 1 lemon 1 teaspoon minced parsley 1 teaspoon sweet herbs (marjoram, sage, thyme) 1 teaspoon salt Freshly ground pepper, to taste 1/4 teaspoon cayenne pepper 2 eggs 3/4 cup breadcrumbs	1. Remove the turkey from packaging and remove the neck and giblets from inside the cavities of the bird. Pat the turkey very dry with paper towels. Season the inside of the turkey with salt and pepper. 2. Tuck the wings of the turkey underneath the bird and set it in a roasting pan. 3. Roast at 325°F for about 13 to 15 minutes per pound or until internal temperature (inserted on middle of thigh and breast) reaches about 165°F. 4. About 20 minutes before the turkey should be done, sprinkle it with flour and then ladle the pan juices over it. Do this two or three times before it's done to make a thin pan gravy. 5. Allow turkey to rest for 20 to 30 minutes before carving. 6. While the turkey is cooking, make the dressing. 7. Chop the bacon into small pieces. Heat the butter in a large frying pan and sauté the bacon for about 5 minutes or until softened. 8. Chop the lemon rind and herbs into small pieces and place in a bowl. Add the salt, pepper, cayenne pepper, and eggs and mix well. Add the breadcrumbs and mix well. 9. Shape into walnut-sized balls and roast on a baking sheet in the oven (while the turkey is resting) for about 30 minutes. This mixture can also be stuffed between the breast meat and skin to cook.

Loin of Pork with Applesauce

This is one of the many dishes that Ethel and the boys would have enjoyed on their journey to America aboard the S.S. *Britannic*. The applesauce recipe can be found on page 58.

Serves 4-6

2-3 pounds boneless pork loin 1 teaspoon salt	1. Trim any excess fat from top of pork loin roast and put into a baking dish. Coat with salt and place in a 425°F oven for 15 minutes. Then reduce heat to 375°F and continue roasting for about 45 minutes or until internal temperature of the pork is 140°F at the center of the roast. 2. Remove from oven and tent pork roast loosely with a piece of foil for 5 to 10 minutes before carving. Serve with applesauce.

Toad in the Hole

Just as Ethel was getting used to doing all the domestic duties on her own, she received a welcomed letter from England. One of the female servants, Gertrude Edith Forster, in their parents' employ was being sent to help her as her pregnancy moved along. She was thrilled to learn that she was getting a domestic servant. Ethel knew they couldn't afford an American one, since they charged one hundred dollars per year. The Chinese men charged sixty dollars per month just to cook. She regretted not having brought Edith with her from the beginning because she had not realized just how much work was involved. So, she quickly penned a letter home with advice on what Edith should bring with her. She wrote, *"She should have quite dark cotton dresses, navy blue or something of that sort; she should have several loose white muslin bodices, a kind of loose dressing jacket, unlined. When the glass is one hundred and twenty in the shade, the cooler clothing one has the better. Also be sure to have sleeves made loose, so that they will roll up. Coloured aprons made of duster stuff are best; they don't look dirty as soon as white. Shoes should be thick, and above all things, all be a size too large. She should have an old ulster to put on the first thing in the morning, to milk in. And remind her to bring a soft pillow, an unattainable luxury out here."*

Ethel was already thinking of the things that Edith could do—washing, milking, cooking, and more. But that day wasn't here yet, and those were still her responsibility. Her family sent her more recipes, and her neighbor, Mr. Brown, slaughtered some of his pigs and sent her a pig's head, of which she made a brawn. She also got sausage meat, liver, and kidneys. She was proud of the fact that she cooked more items than any domestic in England would dream of touching. She did, however, express her main offense of cooking. *"I have not got over my disgust at touching raw meat and especially the 'innards.' The liver was the most repulsive to touch and cut up."*

Serves 4-6

1 1/3 cups flour 1/4 teaspoon salt 1 large egg 1 cup milk 6 pork sausages, cooked 2 tablespoons beef dripping Freshly ground black pepper, to taste	1. Place the flour and salt in a large bowl. Make a well in the middle of the flour and add the eggs. Using a wooden spoon, gradually beat the eggs into the flour, then slowly add in the milk. Mix until you have a slightly thick batter that has no lumps. 2. Cut the sausage into pieces and season with salt and pepper. 3. Place the drippings into a pie pan or ovenproof dish and add the sausages. Pour in the batter and bake at 400°F for about 35 to 40 minutes until puffy and golden.

EDITH: FRIEND & FOE

Ethel received an unexpected surprise with Edith's arrival. Despite Edith being her domestic, they were close in age, and she and her boss developed a close friendship. Back in England, Edith was the hired help, and no matron would think of befriending her maid. However, in the West, women in remote locations could not afford to be choosey with their female companions. Such was the case with Edith and Ethel. Ethel wrote a letter home that no doubt seemed out of place to her aristocratic family back in England. *"I had no idea E.F. was such fun. It's quite delightful to be frivolous again, after so much solitude. I have laughed more in the last fortnight that I have since I left England."*

Edith jumped into her domestic duties, and life in Burns Valley continued to progress. In March, she even participated in a social event at the new hall. Both she and Gerald performed in the operetta musical, *Box and Cox*. Gerald played Cox, while Edith played the small part of Mrs. Bouncer. The premise of the play was Mrs. Bouncer, who was a London lodging-house keeper, letting an apartment to two different men. The first man was Box, who was a printer on a daily newspaper, and the other was Cox, a journeyman hatter. Box occupied the room during the day and Cox did at night. They met on the stairs of the lodging-house when one came in from work as the other is going out. Neither had any idea that Mrs. Bouncer was letting his room to the other. Cox, suspicious that Mrs. Bouncer had been using his flat during the day, complained to her that his coal kept disappearing, and there was *"a steady increase of evaporation among my candles, wood, sugar and Lucifer matches."* He also complained that his room was continually full of tobacco smoke. Mrs. Bouncer gave various excuses—among others, that Box, who, she says, occupied the attic, is a persistent smoker, and that his smoke must come down the chimney. The little comedy performed in Burns Valley took in sixty-one dollars ($1,430), and the local paper even ran a review of it.

Community School Building, ca. 1880s.

MAIN MEALS • 73

GERALD'S SUDDEN DEPARTURE

The July 1894 timing of a telegram that Gerald received seemed oddly suspicious. The papers of the day claimed the sender was anonymous and requested that Gerald return to England immediately for an acting engagement in Hope Booth's *Little Miss Cute*. It included one thousand dollars for his transportation. In fact, Hope Booth stated in an interview that Gerald wrote to her asking for a part in her new play. She immediately sent a reply back and invited him to join her. She stated in August, *"Mr. Gerald Hertslet… the latter gentleman cabled over from America to know if I could find a place in my piece for him, and as a result of my reply, he has just arrived in London."* Ethel was suspicious of the request. It didn't matter to Gerald because he was returning home with the promise of a lucrative theater opportunity in London! Rumors in the papers ran the gamut of him deserting his wife to her being behind the invitation to get him out of the way. However, if Ethel had been behind it, certainly Hope Booth would have mentioned that to Gerald in her response to him. Gerald packed his trunks and once again left his wife alone in early July 1894. He was bound for Southampton via the Panama Canal aboard the Royal West Indian line. Ethel, now alone in America, turned to her cousin Claude.

Across the pond, Gerald made his stage debut on September 14, 1894, at the Royalty Theatre in London in *Little Miss Cute*. It was hardly the Savoy or Haymarket, but it was a stage in London. Its staircase walls were decorated in a period combination of dark red and gold paper, and the interior of the house matched with its red velvet and imitation pearl decor. Gerald's role was the lover of Miss Hope Booth, a flamboyant and risqué American actress. She was born Luella Maud Hope but used the stage name of Hope Booth because she claimed she was the niece of world-renowned thespian Edwin Booth and his brother, assassin John Wilkes Booth.

After three weeks of rehearsing, Gerald stepped onto the stage where over six hundred watched his London debut. Among the notables was his former Lake County neighbor, Lillie Langtry, who had a box for the show. Gerald's English stage career was shorter lived than any of his California ventures. The show opened and closed on the same day. Booth, expecting the show to be a resounding success, leased the theater for six weeks. However, much to her dismay, it failed miserably after opening night. The papers wrote about how awful the play was and that Gerald's bad performance largely contributed to its demise. The *New York Herald* reported, *"Besides Lord Hay… there is another Englishman of alleged aristocratic lineage, who, it is said, set sail. This gentleman is Gerald Hertslet, a son of Sir Edward Hertslet. Gerald was a member of Miss Booth's company under the name of Spencer. It was his first and last appearance on any stage, and it is said that he contributed his full share of effort to the general disaster."* Hope Booth was distraught and in deep debt, so she fled to America. *The Pittsburgh Press* wrote, *"It is my opinion that Miss Hope Booth is swindling the easily-swindled American public with the two noble hangers-on who she reports to be in her train. Of Gerald Hertslet there is more certainty than the other. Sir Edward Hertslet, 'Gerald's' father, is a K.C.B. and so comparatively well known… Lord Hay."*

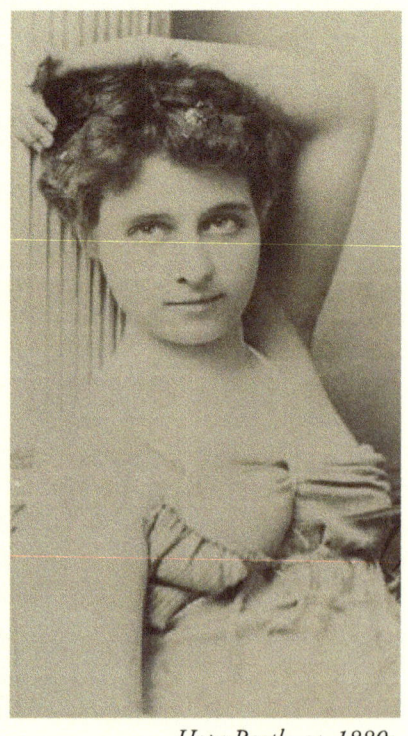

Hope Booth, ca. 1880s.

74 · VICTORIAN RECIPES WITH A SIDE OF SCANDAL

Roast Beef with Gravy

Even though Ethel was given a brief introduction in the basement of her parents' London home, she was still a novice. She noted in a letter home to England, *"We had a roast beef, a sort of joint I never saw before, so I cannot describe it. It was not difficult to cook. I simply put it in a tin in the oven with a pat of butter on its back, and when it was done in about an hour and a half, I took it out and poured a little hot water over it which made the gravy."*

Serves 6

4 to 4 1/2 pounds boneless prime rib Salt, to taste 1/2 cup water	1. Preheat the oven to 390°F. Use paper towels to dry the meat well and sprinkle with salt. Place the beef into a shallow roasting pan and cook for 20 minutes and then reduce the heat to 340°F. Roast another hour for rare beef, 1 hour and 25 minutes for medium, and 1 hour and 45 minutes for well done. 2. Once cooked, remove the meat to a carving board and tent with foil while it rests. 3. Place the pan over medium heat and add the water. Scrape the bottom to remove the fond or bits from the bottom to make a gravy. Slice the meat and serve.

Fried Steak and Onions

Ethel served Gerald and the boys this dish for supper while living on the ranch.

Serves 4

4 sirloin or strip steaks, about 1 1/2 pounds 2 large onions, peeled and sliced 2 tablespoons butter Salt and pepper, to taste	1. Heat a large skillet over medium heat and add 1 tablespoon of the butter and melt. Add the onions and sauté until golden and slightly softened. Remove from the pan and set aside. 2. Melt the remaining butter in the pan over medium high heat and add the steaks, being sure not to crowd the pan or they'll poach. 3. Cook for about 6 minutes for rare, 8 minutes for medium, or longer for more well done. Turn as needed. Remove from the pan and season with salt and pepper. 4. Add the onions back to the pan to reheat quickly while the steaks rest and then place them on top of the steaks.

Chili con Carne

By May 1894, Ethel and Gerald were growing apart, and she and her cousin Claude were spending a great deal of time together, taking walks in the park and attending the Midwinter Fair. The two were almost inseparable, and as they spent more time together, Gerald grew angry. He told Ethel he didn't think it was appropriate for her to be out with Claude until eleven at night. Ethel told him that they were merely cousins spending time together.

The Midwinter Fair was a huge event for San Francisco in 1894 and was conceived by M. H. De Young, who was the owner of the *San Francisco Chronicle*. It was built in the Golden Gate Park where two hundred acres

Main Concourse of the 1894 Midwinter Fair in San Francisco

were cleared, and more than one hundred buildings were completed. Ethel and Claude made up some of the two million people who attended the fair. As they strolled the grounds, they saw exhibits from different states, territories, and foreign countries. There was a variety of architectural styles, including Old Mission, modified Corinthian, Egyptian, Moorish, and East Indian. The exposition emphasized agricultural, horticultural and mineral exhibits, and many new varieties of fruits and grains that were displayed for the first time. Delicacies to sample from home and around the world cost thirty-five to fifty cents, which was quite steep for the event. They had their choice of German dishes from the Heidelberg castle, milk and sandwiches from the Flemish dairy and the Swiss chalet, the Marine restaurant who served freshly caught fish, or the Indian village where "an old woman" cooked tortillas over a Comal. They could also choose Japanese fare where costumed girls served rice and tea, the mining camp who offered beans and a variety of drinks, or the Ceylon booth in the Manufacturer's building, who served coffee and tea by "quaint little Ceylonese men." There were even more choices at the Mexican exhibit where they could sample poi with their fingers in the Hawaiian restaurant or try Mexican tamales and chili con carne.

Serves 4

6 dried red chile peppers, stemmed and seeded	1. Place the peppers in a bowl and cover with boiling water for 1 hour.
Boiling water	2. Pour the peppers and water into a blender, add the flour, and mix until smooth. Pour that into a stock pot and add the remaining ingredients.
1 teaspoon flour	
4 garlic cloves, diced	3. Bring to a boil and then reduce heat to simmer and cook until tender or about 2 to 3 hours. Taste for seasoning.
1 teaspoon salt	
1 medium onion, peeled and diced, optional	
1 8-ounce can tomato sauce, optional	
1 1/2 pounds stew beef	

ETHEL AND CLAUDE FILE FOR DIVORCES

In October 1894, Ethel filed for divorce with her attorney in San Francisco and cited Gerald with infidelity and desertion. With an opportunity to get reader's attention, the Associated Press ran their divorce story. Papers both large and small across the United States, including the *San Francisco Chronicle, Salt Lake Tribune, Arizona Republic, Lock Haven Express* (PA), and many others, ran the story. Some were simply a few lines, while others bore extreme details.

On October 18, Claude filed his own cause. After six years of marriage to Edith, he filed for divorce against his estranged wife. In a male-dominated Victorian era, Claude charged Edith with extreme cruelty toward him starting in 1890 and lasting until the day she walked out.

He claimed her actions had caused him great mental suffering, and during that entire time she was a morphine addict. He claimed she used such large quantities and was so addicted, that at times she remained stupefied and was unable to "discharge" her domestic and marital duties. As if that wasn't enough, he filed a second and separate cause which cited that in addition to her morphine addiction, Edith had been debilitated from her household and marital duties from using intoxicating liquors. Claude also noted that a year earlier Edith tried to stab him with a knife while she was under the influence. But, being larger than his stoned wife, he was able to fight her off.

She filed a cross-complaint denying the accusations and to stop the divorce. In the end, Claude was required to pay his wife twenty dollars per month in alimony. After a few months of not getting any money from him, Edith filed a complaint. He was cited to appear before Judge Troutt to show cause why he did not pay the alimony and was charged twenty dollars in court cost, fifty dollars in counsel fees in the divorce proceedings against Gertrude Edith Barry. He never showed.

Edith recalled her version of the events that led up to the divorces including when she arrived in America, married Claude, how they all went to San Francisco, and how she and Claude agreed to split up under amicable terms. Even some of the details of this story, told by Edith, are incorrect, including the dates both she and Claude arrived. It's not known whether Edith embellished the story for sympathy or the newspaper just got it wrong.

She continued her story in true Victorian fashion with a flair for drama. *"On my filing of a cross-complaint… my husband, now recognizing that I would fight him to the bitter end, one day disappeared from this city. All I heard of him was the fact of his starvation to death in New York City, a fate he richly deserves."* She claims they were never divorced, but if that were true, why would Claude have had to appear in court in 1895 to pay alimony? She stated that at first Claude and Ethel hid their relationship in San Francisco but then openly displayed it—even passing her in the street without recognition. She continued with her melodramatic prose, *"Through Claude Barry's negligence I have been sick nigh unto death (having spent weeks in the hospital), with the barest necessities of life as my portion, and I can but bitterly denounce the duplicity of a man who promised to care for me in life."* This was the last trace of public information that can be located for Gertrude Edith Forster Barry.

MAIN MEALS • 77

Mutton Stew

Ethel continued acting after Gerald went back to England and toured successfully until she left for Canada and then New York City, where she and Claude met up. When they found themselves in New York City without employment in the late 1890s, their meals were small and lean. One of them was mutton stew and bread.

This is a copy of a playbill from *The Tarrytown Widow,* in which Ethel played on December 5, 1898 in North Adams, Massachusetts. She played the maiden aunt, Miss Ann Morris at the Wilson Opera House.

It was a four-act play about elderly Benjamin Bascom, who is a married man who tries to flirt with a pretty widow and finds himself involved in an affair of the heart with a hideous and vociferous spinster. *The North Adams Evening Transcript* reported the troupe was from fresh off their success at the Bijou Theater in New York City. The comedy was written by Charles Dazey and originally opened on May 9, 1898, at the Bijou.

On Valentine's Day in 1899 the *Boston Journal* wrote, *"…Ethel Hertslet as the maiden aunt was capital."* The *Boston Daily Globe* also wrote, *"Miss Ethel Hertslet deserves praise for her performance in an eccentric character role."*

The play closed that night after a fire destroyed most of the set and costumes.

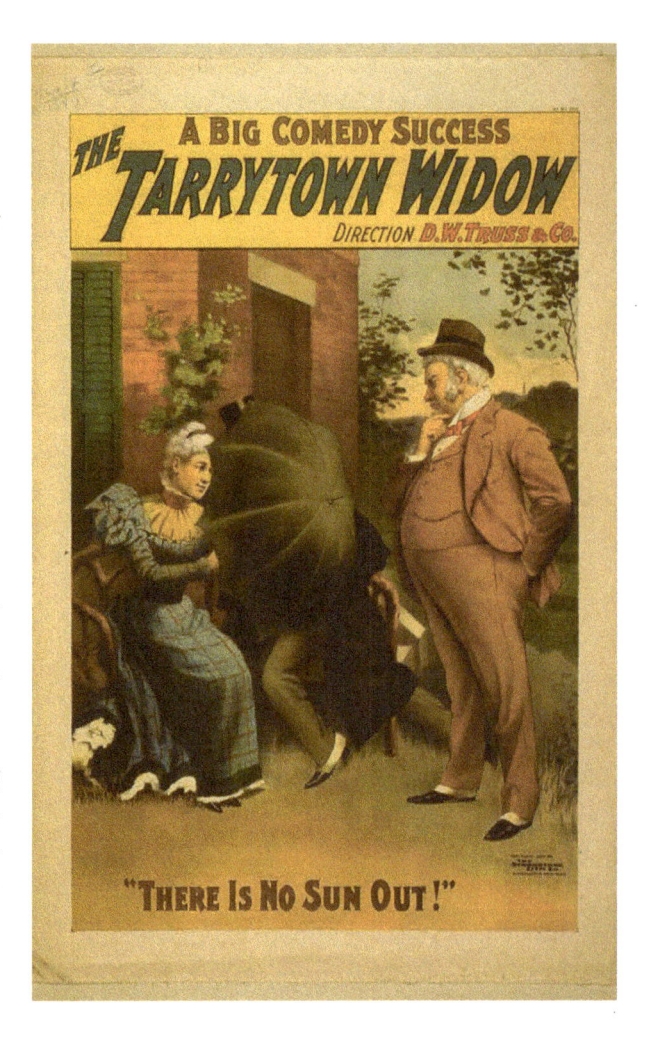

Serves 4

1 pound mutton or stew beef 2 ounces butter 1 onion, peeled and sliced 1 ounce flour 1 1/2 cups beef broth 1 carrot, chopped 1/2 turnip or potato, chopped Salt and pepper, to taste	1. Melt butter over medium high heat in a large stock pot. Add the meat and quickly fry until browned. Remove. Add the onion and cook until golden and then add the flour. Stir to coat the onions and cook for about 2 minutes. Add the stock and bring to a boil. Add the meat, carrot, turnip, and seasonings to the pot. Stir. Reduce heat to simmer and cover. Cook for 1 to 2 hours or until the meat is tender. Taste for seasoning.

Mutton Cutlets

Before all the drama ensued later in her life, Ethel enjoyed entertaining at her ranch, even if she had to do all the work herself. While preparing for a supper with the Keatinges, Ethel opened her cooking books and found recipes for salmon cakes, beet-root and cream, and mutton cutlets.

Serves 4-6

4 mutton chops 1/2 teaspoon salt 1/2 teaspoon freshly ground pepper 1 cup dry breadcrumbs 2 eggs, beaten Butter for frying Lemon slices and chives, for garnish	1. Wash and pat the chops dry. Sprinkle both sides with salt and pepper. Dredge the chops in the eggs and then through the bread crumbs. 2. Melt the butter over medium-high heat and add the cutlets. Cook until golden brown on both sides or about 15 minutes. Pierce with a fork to see if the juices run clear. 3. Garnish with lemon and chives.

Dressed Crab

This is one of the many dishes onboard the R.M.S. *Etruria*. See the ice cream entry on page 99 for the story behind this recipe.

Serves 1

1 crab, cooked 2 tablespoons vinegar 2 tablespoons oil 1/2 teaspoon mustard 1/4 teaspoon salt 1/4 teaspoon white pepper Cayenne pepper, to taste	1. Pick the meat from the crab and empty the body of the shell. Meanwhile, mix the crab meat and remaining ingredients. 2. Place the mixture back into the shell and serve with fresh lemon and parsley. 3. Pre-picked crabmeat may be used and served on a plate.

Pickled Oysters

This is another of the many dishes offered on the R.M.S. *Etruria* that Ethel may have enjoyed on her 1905 journey to England from New York.

Serves 2-4

2 dozen raw oysters 1/3 cup retained oyster liquor, strained 1/2 cup vinegar pinch of nutmeg 1 pinch celery salt 1 teaspoon salt Pinch of paprika 1 bay leaf 10 to 12 peppercorns 6 allspice berries 3 cloves	1. Thoroughly rinse and shuck the oysters (skip if using canned). As they are shucked, retain all the liquor in the shell. Once finished, strain the liquor through a fine mesh strainer or cheese cloth. 2. Place the oysters, liquor, vinegar, nutmeg, salts, and paprika in a sauce pan. 3. Tie up the bay leaf, peppercorns, allspice, and cloves in a piece of cheese cloth or place into a loose-leaf tea infuser. Add to the pan with the oysters and cook on medium low heat. When the liquid reaches a boil, remove from the heat and place into glass canning jars with the liquid. Seal the jars and allow to cool slightly before placing the jars in the refrigerator. The oysters will be ready in 2 days and should be used within 4.

DESSERTS

COMPOTE OF PEARS 83

TIPSY CAKE 84

SPONGE CAKE 85

VICTORIA SANDWICHES 87

SIMNEL CAKE 88

BREAD & BUTTER PUDDING 89

PLUM PUDDING 90

CORNSTARCH PUDDING 91

CUSTARD PUDDING 92

MINCE PIE 93

MINCEMEAT 93

PIE CRUST 94

MERINGUES 94

GRANDMA NITA'S MARSHMALLOW FUDGE 96

GRANDMA NITA'S ENGLISH TOFFEE 97

ICE CREAM 99

R.M.S. ETRURIA

The R.M.S. *Etruria,* launched in 1884, was a crown jewel of the Cunard Line, epitomizing the competitive spirit of the transatlantic shipping industry in the late 19th century. As one of the last major Cunard liners to feature auxiliary sails alongside its powerful steam engine, the *Etruria* represented a transitional period in maritime technology. With a gross tonnage of 7,718 and a service speed of 19 knots, it was among the fastest ships of its era, earning the prestigious Blue Riband for the fastest westbound crossing in 1885.

The *Etruria* was designed with an emphasis on both speed and luxury, catering to the demands of wealthy travelers and emigrants heading to the United States. Its interiors featured opulent first-class accommodations, including richly decorated staterooms, plush lounges, and elegant dining facilities. The second-class accommodations, though less extravagant, were also comfortable, and the ship's spacious design ensured that even third-class passengers experienced a level of service superior to many contemporaries.

What set the *Etruria* apart was its role as a pioneer in technological and social advancements. Its engines, a marvel of engineering for their time, were capable of generating immense power, propelling the vessel swiftly across the often-turbulent Atlantic. Simultaneously, the ship served as a stage for the vibrant mix of cultures and classes traveling to the New World, reflecting the transformative era of global migration.

Contemporary illustration of R.M.S. Etrutia, *ca. 1900.*

The *Etruria's* reputation wasn't without incident, however. In 1903, it collided with a coal ship, though no lives were lost, and the liner was swiftly repaired. The following year, the ship experienced a notable mutiny among its crew, an event that highlighted the intense labor conditions aboard such vessels. Despite these challenges, the Etruria maintained a steady service life until its retirement in 1908.

Although eventually overshadowed by newer and grander Cunard liners like the *Lusitania* and *Mauretania,* the *Etruria* was a symbol of ambition and innovation, bridging the gap between the age of sail and the dominance of steam, while leaving an indelible mark on maritime history.

Compote of Pears

This is one of the desserts Ethel and the boys may have enjoyed in their journey to America aboard the S.S. *Britannic*.

Serves 4

- 1 cup sugar
- 1 cup water
- 2 whole cloves
- 2 allspice berries
- 6 ripe pears, peeled and cored

1. Place the sugar, water, and spices into a sauce pan large enough to hold the pears. Heat the mixture over medium heat until it becomes slightly thickened, or about 10 minutes. Add the pears and cook until tender or about 20 to 30 minutes.
2. Remove the pears and drain on a towel. Allow the syrup to cook until it reduces and becomes thick or about 3 minutes. Allow the pears and syrup to completely cool. Remove cloves and allspice berries from the syrup. Place the pears in a shallow serving dish and pour the syrup over them.

Tipsy Cake

Ethel seemed fairly happy about her first Christmas as a rancher's wife and became very excited about making her first Christmas Day dinner. On Christmas morning in 1885, they hoped to have a small service at the hall, but again, the weather prevented that, so they headed home so Ethel could begin Christmas dinner for eleven people. Miss May joined them to keep Ethel company and not be the only woman and also helped Ethel clean up. She set the table with her China and placed manzanita flowers on it for decoration. They had just come into bloom and perfumed the air. She poured the wine, placed the dishes on the table, and they all sat down to eat. Not surprisingly, she was thrilled with the success of her Christmas dinner. *"Now you really must hear about my Christmas dinner. The plum pudding and mince pies were all that could be desired, and we had also tipsy cake, Victoria sandwiches, meringues, and dessert."* Ethel had only been in America for seven short months, so the comments she made about dinner service is not surprising, *"…it seemed so funny having to dish up and then sit down to dinner, and after dinner have to wash up… I am sure it didn't look much like 'roughing it' in California! There were eleven of us all together, and we were a very merry party and drank to everyone's health 'at home.'"* By now she was about five months pregnant and penned, *"You can't think how glad I am that Christmas is over, and I feel rather a wreck; but as the dinner was an undoubted success, I rest happy."*

Makes 1 cake

1 Bundt-size sponge cake, stale 3/4 cup brandy 3/4 cup sherry 1 cup almond slivers, blanched 2 cups custard	1. Place the cake in a deep dish and poke holes all around the cake. 2. Blend sherry and brandy together and pour over cake. Stick the almonds all over the cake, then cover it with your favorite custard. 3. Place in a cool place and allow cake to soak for 2 hours before serving.

84 · VICTORIAN RECIPES WITH A SIDE OF SCANDAL

Sponge Cake

Makes 1 cake

- 2 cups flour
- 1/2 teaspoon salt
- 2 tablespoons lemon juice
- 10 egg whites
- 2 teaspoons grated lemon rind
- 1 1/4 cups sugar
- 10 egg yolks

1. Sift the flour and salt in a large bowl and set aside.
2. Beat the egg yolks until thick and yellow. Add the lemon juice and rind and blend well.
3. In a separate bowl, beat the egg whites until soft peaks form. While whipping, gradually add the sugar and continue beating until stiff peaks form.
4. Gently fold in the egg yolks and then the flour, 1/4 cup at a time. Be sure not to over beat this mixture, or the cake will not rise properly.
5. Pour batter into an ungreased 10-inch bundt pan and bake at 350° for 1 hour.
6. Invert the cake pan on a plate, and allow to cool for 1 hour before removing the pan from the cake.
7. Be sure to cut the cake with a serrated knife so that you do not flatten it.

ETHEL BECOMES A MOTHER

As Ethel's due date grew near, she tried to hire a nursemaid to come to her house, but no one wanted the job. Knowing she needed someone to help her give birth to her first child, they decided to go into the town of Vallejo, California. On March 31, they traveled the rough forty-mile drive to Calistoga in their wagon, and they took their own horses and went slow. Their hired helper and Edith, paid them a course of short visits so she could wash and bake for them. Ethel and Gerald arrived in Vallejo on April 1, and on April 3, 1886, Jolette Edith Hertslet was born to two very happy parents. Five days after that, they celebrated their first anniversary.

Traditionally, both Ethel and Gerald's family named their children after relatives, so why they chose the name Jolette for their daughter is a mystery. Ethel's descendants have a theory about the name, which has been passed down through the generations, including Jolette herself! The story is that Ethel was enamored with someone named Joe in California, so Jolette means little Jo. To date, no one named Joe has been located or associated with Ethel in any research. Jolette is also a version of Juliet, which Ethel reportedly played when Gerald first met her. Despite why that name was chosen, Jolette was given the middle name of Edith, which was both Ethel's mother's name and her live-in domestic's. Ethel was so proud of her new baby and wrote, *"She is, fortunately, the best of babies and lies awake and placid for hours in the hammock while I am busy."* Ethel was also proud of a compliment she received from a visitor, *"…he was so pleased with the cheerful look of our kitchen and bright range and complimented me on baby's appearance, remarking that she looked so well cared for, which remark pleased me, considering how hard I have to work to keep her nice."*

Jolette Edith Hertslet in 1898 at the age of 12.

86 · VICTORIAN RECIPES WITH A SIDE OF SCANDAL

Victoria Sandwiches

One of the desserts that Ethel served while living on the ranch in Lake County included this traditional English dish with "sugar icing." When Queen Victoria's birthday arrived on May 24, 1885, Ethel and about twenty other English ex-pats gathered for a birthday party in her honor where they all sang "God Save the Queen." Ethel wrote home about their celebration. *"I wonder if she would have been edified if she could have seen us all, in this little wooden house, singing away so heartily."* Ethel's friends and British Consulate George Stanley also organized a party in San Francisco for the Queen. Gerald was a member of the British Benevolent Society, and they held their nineteenth annual celebration with a picnic, games, races, and music. They all sang Tennyson's English and Colonial song, "Hands All Around," as the music was performed by the U.S. Artillery Band.

Serves 4-6

Butter, equal to the weight of the eggs Sugar, equal to the weight of the eggs 4 eggs (weigh them in their shells) Flour, equal to the weight of the eggs 1/4 teaspoon salt Jam or marmalade, any kind	1. Cream the butter for about 5 minutes, then add the sugar and beat for 2 to 3 minutes. Add the eggs and beat for 3 minutes. Add the flour and salt and beat for an additional 5 minutes. 2. Butter a 9 x 9-inch baking tin and pour in the batter. Bake at 350°F for 20 to 25 minutes. Use a toothpick to test for doneness. 3. Allow to cool on a cake rack. Cut the cake in half and spread the jam on the bottom half of the cake. Place the other half of the cake on top and gently press the pieces together. Cut them into long finger-pieces. Pile them in crossbars on a glass dish and serve.

Simnel Cake

While Ethel was living in Lake County, she often recalled her home in England and the adventures she had traveling around Europe. It was 1885 when she wrote, *"I pine for a Buszard's cake."* Buszard's was well-known for its cakes and confections but especially their "bride" cakes. They were located on Oxford Street in London and were described in a newspaper, "Buszard's establishment is literally an emporium of wedding-cakes and of the delectable meats of which they are composed. One's eye there rests upon rows of these precious emblems of affection, ranging from the wedding-cake designed for a princess to the less expensive cake manufactured to meet the tastes of one to middle fortune born. There is no other shop in London, as far as we are aware, devoted so exclusively to one specialty. The wedding-cakes of Messrs. Buszard are sent to all parts of the world. It is no uncommon thing for an order to come from Paris, the city of all others where one might suppose the confectioner's art had attained the highest state of perfection. 'Buszard's' is a favourite resort of ladies during the season. They go there to eat ices, the while, no doubt, they ponder the (let us hope) pleasant recollections which crowd around wedding-cakes already eaten, and anticipate with joy a wedding-cake or two yet to be cut." They stayed in business until their premises were irretrievably damaged during the Second World War. They enjoyed a short post-war revival at 496-500 Oxford Street but disappeared in the 1950s. Simnel cake is a traditional Easter or Mother's Day cake.

Serves 8-12

3/4 cup butter 3/4 cup sugar 3 eggs, beaten 2 1/2 cups flour Pinch salt 3/4 teaspoon ground mixed spice (cinnamon, allspice, mace, and cloves) 1 cup currants, dusted in flour 1 orange, grated peel 1 lemon, grated peel 1/2 cup brandy 6 drops yellow food color Almond paste, optional Icing, optional	1. Cream the butter and sugar together until pale and fluffy. Gradually beat in the eggs until well incorporated and then sift in the flour, salt, and mixed spices. Next, add the mixed dried fruit, citrus zest, brandy, and food coloring to the mixture. 2. Put the mixture into a well-greased 8-inch cake pan. Smooth the top and leave a slight dip in the center to allow for the cake to rise. Bake in a preheated 350°F oven for 1 3/4 hours. Test by inserting a toothpick in the middle, and if it comes out clean, then it's done. Remove from the oven and set aside to cool on a wire rack. 3. Optionally, the cake can be covered with an almond paste and then topped with regular icing. To do this, roll out almond paste to the shape of the cake and place on top and then place the frosting all over the cake. Small balls can also be shaped from the almond paste and added to the top for decoration. Note: They made their food color by saffron threads.

Bread & Butter Pudding

Back in 1885 when they crossed the Atlantic to America on S.S. *Britannic,* Ethel and the boys enjoyed treats like gooseberry and bread and butter pudding, Nelson cakes, marmalade tartlets, and chocolate creams. After their meals, Ethel could retire to her room or to visit the women's saloon to chat with other ladies. The boys could make their way to the smoking room where other men gathered. That was their routine for the ten days.

Serves 6-8

9 slices of thin bread	1. Butter the bread on both sides and cover the bottom of a 9-inch pie pan. Add the currants on top and over with the rest of the buttered bread.
Butter for spreading on the bread	
3 cups milk or cream	2. Beat the eggs in a bowl and add the milk and sugar and stir until blended. Pour over the bread and press down to make sure it gets soaked well.
4 eggs	
1/4 to 1/2 cup sugar or to taste	3. Bake at 350°F for about 35 to 45 minutes or until the middle is set.
3/4 cup dried currants, cranberries, or raisins	4. Serve warm or cold.
1 teaspoon vanilla	

Plum Pudding

Plum pudding is a traditional English dessert that goes back centuries. Ethel and her Lake County English neighbors often served it for special occasions, including Christmas.

Serves 6-8

2 cups stale bread 2 cups milk 1 egg, beaten 1/4 cup molasses 1/4 cup sugar 6 tablespoons butter, melted 1/2 cup raisins, prunes, or a combination 1/2 teaspoon salt 1/4 teaspoon of cinnamon, cloves, and mace 1/4 teaspoon ground nutmeg 1/2 teaspoon chopped orange peel 1 cup brandy	1. Remove the crusts from the bread and cut or shred the bread into small pieces and lay on a baking sheet. Bake at 300°F until dry or about 10 minutes, depending upon how dry the bread was to start. Place the bread in a large bowl and cover with the milk. Let stand for about an hour or until the milk is absorbed and soft. 2. Beat the bread and milk until combined and then add the eggs, butter, molasses, salt, raisins, spices, and orange peel. 3. Grease a 2-quart oven-proof dish. Fill the greased pan half full of batter. Cover with lids or heavy-duty aluminum foil. Bake at 300°F for 2 hours. Test with a knife, and if it comes out clean when put into center of pudding, it's done. 4. Pour brandy over the pudding and allow to cool. Refrigerate until ready to eat.

Roland Brown's house, where Ethel and the boys stayed until they build their home nearby. ca 1880s.

Corn Starch Pudding

While on her California ranch, Ethel would not let the boys do any cooking and wrote home, *"I will not let them in the sacred precincts of my kitchen. Men always make slops when they cook. I have found that the little* Kensington School of Cookery *book very useful because it is so simple. Mr. Brown has a packet of papers from Kensington telling in the most minute way how to cook things. I wish you could send me some, particularly for puddings. There is no suet to be had, and very little drippings, as the meat is baked. We buy lard in tins. They have mush and eggs for breakfast, meat and pudding for dinner, and eggs and cakes, or perhaps cold meat, for supper."*

Serves 6

4 tablespoons corn starch 2 cups milk 3 tablespoons powdered sugar 2 eggs 1/2 cinnamon stick 1/2 teaspoon freshly grated nutmeg	1. Put the corn starch in a large mixing bowl and add a tablespoon of the milk; stir until smooth. Set aside. 2. Place the remaining milk into a saucepan with the sugar and cinnamon stick. Heat the mixture over medium heat until the milk gently boils. Whisk the milk mixture into the cornstarch slurry and stir until smooth. Remove the cinnamon stick. 3. While whisking, add the eggs to the mixture and beat lightly. 4. Grease a quart pie pan with butter and pour the mixture into the pan. Grate half a teaspoon of nutmeg over the top. 5. Bake at 220°F for 30 minutes. A knife will come out clean when done. Serve hot or cold.

DESSERTS · 91

Custard Pudding

Ethel spent a lot of time making desserts or "puddings" as they were called in England. This custard "pudding," aka pie, is another one of her culinary triumphs. As the boys planted and planned in 1885, Ethel was relieved that her cow Becky was no longer being half-starved. Gerald finally purchased five tons of wheat hay, and Becky started receiving a full diet. Once that happened, she began producing about five quarts of milk per day, and Ethel was able to make butter. Ethel loved milking her cow, but Becky proved frustrating for her on several occasions. Becky had a mind of her own and often wandered away and went missing for days. At first, Ethel found it amusing, but she grew frustrated with Becky because she did not have milk or butter when she wandered off. When Becky wasn't missing, she waited outside the door for Ethel, who headed out to milk her with pails swinging in each hand. Her pet lamb Bimbi and her three cats all followed. As Ethel milked, the hungry kittens sat meowing, so she held one up and squirted milk into its mouth. She frequently made dessert milk puddings when Becky was producing milk.

Ethel's furry clan grew to include a sheep dog named Nick, Rags the ranch dog, Bimbi the lamb, Baldy the old cat, and Huz and Buz, the kittens. She called them her happy family and thought them amusing. She enjoyed how they all ate from the same bowl together and how the kittens became very fond of Bimbi. One day, much to her distress, Ethel found one of her kittens near death. She promptly gave it a dose of brandy, and after being intoxicated for a few hours, the kitten jumped up and made a full recovery. She wrote, *"…it got up and lurched about the kitchen in the most absurd way and finally recovered."* See the Pie Crust recipe on page 94.

Serves 8

3 eggs 3 tablespoons sugar 1/8 teaspoon salt 1 1/4 cups milk, half and half, or cream Nutmeg, freshly grated 1 8-inch pie crust	1. In a large bowl, beat the eggs. Add the sugar, salt, and milk and beat until light and fluffy. 2. Pour the custard into the pie crust and sprinkle the top with freshly grated nutmeg. 3. Bake at 450°F for 10 minutes and then reduce the heat to 350°F. Continue cooking for an additional 40 to 50 minutes or until a knife inserted comes out clean. 4. Allow to cool completely before cutting. Chilling the pie enhances the flavors. 5. See recipe for pie crust on another page.

Mince Pie

Of course, no traditional English holiday would be complete without a proper mince pie, which Ethel served at her first Christmas dinner in Lake County in 1885.

Serves 8

2 1/2 cups mincemeat 1 double pie crust, unbaked	1. Line a 9-inch pie pan with 1 pie crust, fill with the mincemeat mixture, and cover with the second pie crust. Pinch the dough together and flute the edges. Bake at 400°F for 35 to 40 minutes or until golden brown. Serve hot.

Mincemeat

Of course, no traditional English holiday would be complete without a proper mince pie, which Ethel served at her first Christmas dinner in Lake County in 1885.

Makes about 4 quarts

1 1/2 pounds lean beef, cubed 1 cup beef stock 1/4 pound lard or shortening 1 pound brown sugar 3 pounds tart apples, peeled and cored 1 cup cider vinegar 2 1/2 pounds raisins 1 cup molasses 1/4 cup candied lemon peel 1 1/2 teaspoons ground cloves 1 tablespoon freshly grated nutmeg 1/2 teaspoon allspice 1 tablespoon cinnamon 1 1/2 teaspoons salt	1. Put meat in a large pot, cover with water, and simmer until tender. Push the meat, lard or shortening, and apples through a food chopper. Place the chopped mixture back in the pot, add remaining ingredients, and simmer for 1 hour, stirring often. The mixture can be canned or used immediately. 2. Note: You can make the mincemeat without meat, just skip the first three ingredients, chop the apples, and combine with the other ingredients and simmer the remaining ingredients for an hour.

Pie Crust

This was often referred to in old recipe books as pie paste or puff paste. This pie crust can be used for either the sweet or savory pie recipes in this book. It can be used to make pies, tarts, or tartlets.

Makes 1 double 9-inch pie crust

2 cups flour 1 1/2 teaspoons baking powder 1/4 teaspoon salt 1 cup cold butter or lard 1 egg 1/4 teaspoon vinegar Cold water	1. Combine the flour, baking powder, and salt in a large mixing bowl. Stir with a wire whisk to combine. Cut in the butter or lard with a pastry cutter and blend until the dough resembles crumbs. 2. Break the egg into a liquid measuring cup and beat lightly. Add the vinegar and enough water to measure 1/3 cup. Stir well. Add the liquid to the flour and shortening mixture. Stir only enough to moisten and combine; overmixing will result in a tough crust. If the dough seems too wet, add a little more flour. 3. Divide the dough in half and roll out on a floured surface. 4. Note: To make a sweeter crust, add 1 tablespoon sugar and 1/2 teaspoon cinnamon to the flour mix. You can cut this recipe in half to make a single crust.

Meringues

This was one of the many desserts that Ethel served at her first Christmas dinner in Lake County in 1885.

Makes About 24 Pieces

4 egg whites 1 cup sugar 1/2 teaspoon vanilla, optional	1. Place the egg whites in a large bowl and allow them to come to room temperature before beating. 2. Beat with an electric mixer on medium-high speed until soft peaks form. Slowly add sugar, about 1 tablespoon at a time, until all the sugar has been added. Continue beating until the whites are stiff and glossy. If using vanilla, add it now and beat for 30 seconds more. 3. Preheat oven to 200°F. Line 2 large baking sheets with parchment paper. Place about a tablespoon of meringue onto the paper and shape it like an egg or a round shape. Space each one about 2 inches apart. 4. Note: This can also be done with a piping bag. 5. Place in the oven and bake until dry and crisp throughout, about 1 1/2 hours. Transfer the meringues to wire racks and let them cool to room temperature.

THE SCANDALOUS DIVORCE

It was June 22, 1898, and Ethel had every intention of appearing before Judge Edwin Nash of the New York Supreme Court to defend herself. When that day came, she never showed, and the divorce went uncontested. It only took a day for the blistering news to hit the papers. It wasn't the first time she saw her name in the paper over this whole affair, but this was New York. Between the *Times* and the *World,* everyone in the city would know all the sordid details. It seemed like her personal life was all that was happening in America. Sadly, for Ethel, even the Spanish American War that was raging on couldn't hide her story. Her ex-husband Gerald didn't purposely seek out to have their personal life appear in the papers, but he was an English Baronet's son, and anything with the Hertslet name was big news. Besides, he had run back to England on an all-expense paid acting gig back in 1892. What did it matter to him that the New York papers ran his name? He wasn't there to feel the effects, but Ethel was.

When the owner of the *New York Times* coined the phrase, "All the news that fit to print," Ethel probably didn't think it meant *her* news. Yet, there it was, on the front page of the June 23 *New York Times*, for all of its seventy-six thousand readers to see. The story was even given prominence in the first column. *"Gerald Spencer Hertslet, son of Sir Edwin [Edward] Hertslet, a prominent Englishman, has been granted a divorce from his wife by the Supreme Court of New York State."* At least the paper saved her details for page four, which included her full name and the fact that Gerald was divorcing her because of infidelity. Fortunately for Ethel, the story did not include all the sordid details like some of the other papers included.

Papers like the *Chicago Tribune, Salt Lake Tribune* and the *San Francisco Chronicle* had no qualms in printing all the personal details, like their failures at ranching and acting in California. Those divorce details ripped their way through some of the nation's largest newspapers and a host of small-town papers. Newspapermen knew the Hertslet name was held in high esteem in England and made for compelling copy. Even the Western Associated Press picked up their story because Gerald descended from a long line of men who had close ties to England's monarchs since 1795. Four generations of Hertslet men held positions in the Foreign Office including Librarian, British Consuls, and Vice Consuls around the world. Their life's successes and failures were often shared with world.

Before it became final though, their divorce languished for three long years as she and Gerald battled using their attorneys as pawns. Accusations were hurled from both sides—some true and some not. Finally, after thirteen years of marriage, that chapter of her life was finally over. But Gerald still influenced her future. Even though he could remarry as if she were dead, she couldn't marry until Gerald actually was dead. On top of that, he gained sole custody of their three children who were living in England.

Grandma Nita's Marshmallow Fudge

Grandma Nita was a little girl Ethel knew as Manzanita Beakbane, whose parents were close friends with the Hertslets in Lake County, California. Both Ethel and Margaret Beakbane had babies in 1889. On July 14, 1889, Ethel gave birth to her third and final child, whom they named Harold Cecil. Margaret gave birth to her second daughter, Manzanita, on October 26, 1889, who was named after the flourishing perfumed Manzanita shrub, whose flowers look like little snowdrops. This is Manzanita Beakbane's fudge recipe that was shared by her granddaughter.

Makes About 4 Pounds

4 cups white sugar 14 ounces evaporated milk 1 stick or 1/2 cup butter 2 pkgs. (12 ounces each) chocolate chips 1 square bitter chocolate, cut fine 2 cups marshmallow whip 1 cup chopped nuts 1 teaspoon vanilla	1. Combine sugar, milk, and butter in a large pot. Heat over medium heat and cook until it reaches 230°F, stirring constantly. 2. Place the chocolate chips, chocolate, and marshmallow whip into a large bowl. 3. Pour the boiling syrup over it and stir well. When mixed completely, add the nuts and vanilla. 4. Put in a buttered 13 x 9-inch pan. Let cool and cut into squares.

Margaret Beakbake with her daughters, Manzanita on the left and Margaret on the right, circa 1880s in Lower Lake, California.

Grandma Nita's English Toffee

The married women who lived in Lake County, California, took turns hosting bachelor dinners, and at the end of September 1885, Margaret Beakbane hosted it. Gerald's brothers, Louis and Bernard, along with friend Henry Brandram rode over to the Beakbanes to attend. That left Ethel and Gerald alone, so Ethel prepared a little tête-à-tête supper for them, and they enjoyed their first private meal together since their three-day honeymoon in London. The Beakbanes' eldest daughter, Manzanita Beakbane-Allen, later lived in Charter Oak in southern California and was known for her candy making she provided for various fundraising bazaars. This is her traditional English toffee recipe that was shared by her granddaughter.

Makes About 3 Pounds.

3 sticks or 1 1/2 cups butter 2 cups sugar 1/2 cup water 1 teaspoon vanilla 12 ounces chocolate, melted English walnuts, medium ground	1. Start by coating two cookie sheets with parchment paper. 2. Place the butter into a heavy 3-quart saucepan and cook over medium heat until almost melted. Next, add the sugar and water, trying not to get the sugar on the edges of the pot. 3. Turn the heat up to medium high and stir for the next 10 minutes or so with a sturdy wooden spoon. Cook until boiling hard. Then add butter, a little at a time, so that the boiling can continue. Boil to a hard ball stage or 300°F on a candy thermometer. Take off the stove quickly and spread thinly onto the sheets. 4. Spread half the melted chocolate on top of toffee, and then sprinkle with half of the English walnuts. Flip the toffee over onto the cookie sheet and spread with the other half of the melted chocolate and nuts. This toffee is meant to be very thin and covered with chocolate and nuts on both sides. 5. Let cool in the pans for 1 to 2 hours. Break into pieces and serve or store.

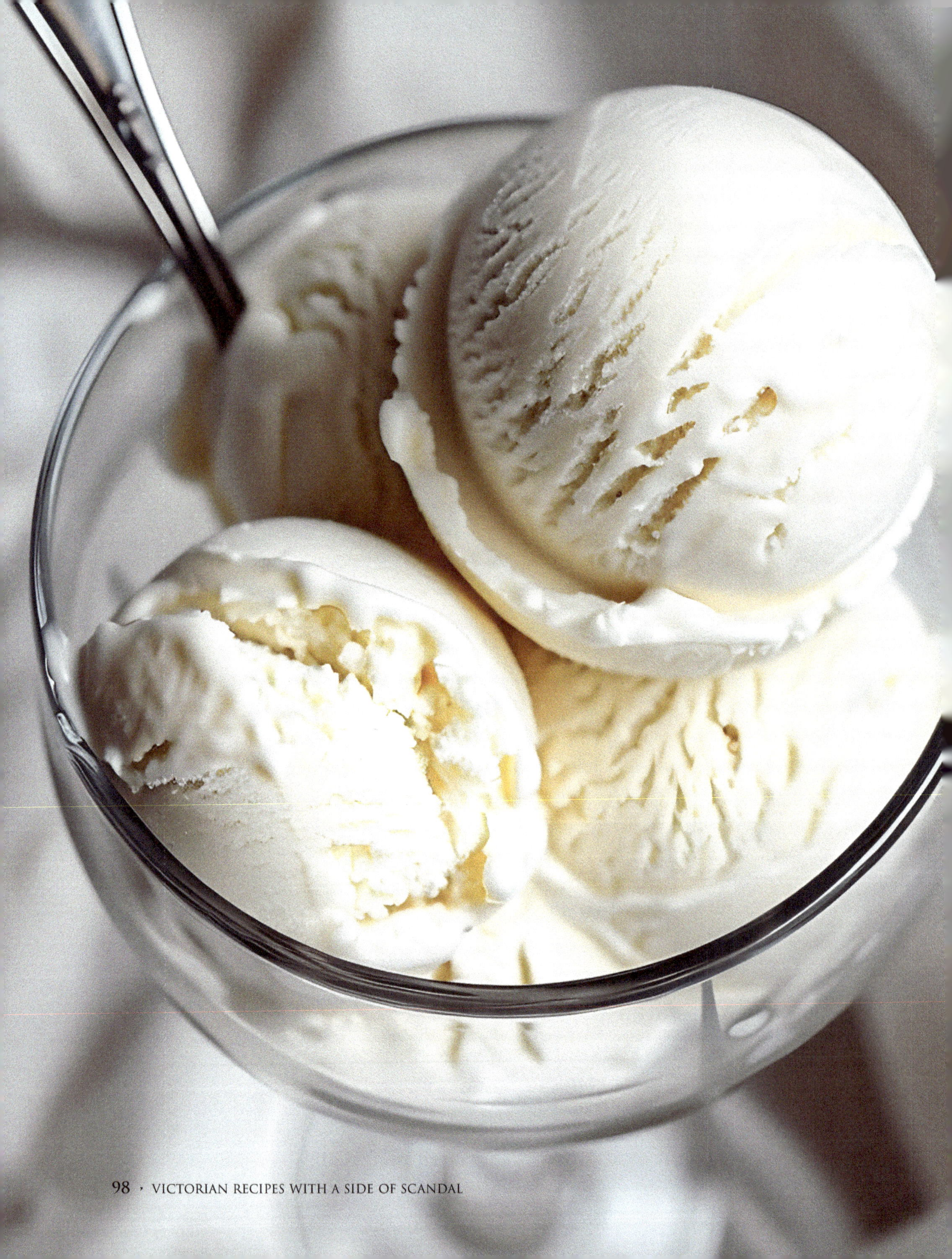

Ice Cream

Ethel had a long acting career in America, but in 1905, it was nearing its end. After performing with Charles Hawtrey's troupe for years, she boarded Cunard's R.M.S. *Etruria* on May 27 from New York to England in hopes of pursuing her career, leaving Claude alone in New York. She, of course, traveled first-class in the Saloon and was only one of twenty-five first-class travelers who enjoyed the ornately carved furniture and heavy velvet curtains that hung in all the public areas. The Cunard luxury liner epitomized the opulent Edwardian style with five hundred first class cabins that were situated on the Promenade, Upper, Saloon, and Main Decks. There was a music room, a smoking room for the gentleman, and separate dining rooms for first and second-class passengers.

Unfortunately for Ethel, she chose to become an actress at the soon-to-be end of an era. Morality and the scenes of daily life, news events, and the worn-out dramatic and comic situations that had become the standard fare began to bore audiences as early as 1900. On top of that, an organization of vaudeville performers called the White Rats of America went on strike and forced many theaters to show motion pictures to fill their bills. This is one of the many dishes offered on the *Etruria*.

Makes 1 1/2 quarts

1 3/4 cups heavy cream 1 1/4 cups whole milk 3/4 cup sugar 1 vanilla bean, split down the middle or 1 teaspoon extract	1. Place cream into a saucepan and add the sugar. If using a bean, add it now. If you want the dark specks from the vanilla bean, scrape out the seeds and add to the mixture. Warm the mixture over medium heat, just until the sugar dissolves. Remove from the heat and add milk and vanilla extract (if using extract). Stir to combine and chill in the refrigerator. 2. When ready to churn, remove the vanilla bean, whisk mixture again, and pour into ice cream maker. 3. Freeze according to ice cream machine instructions.

R.M.S. Etruria, ca. 1905.

DESSERTS • 99

ETHEL THE ACTRESS

Ethel played various characters in farce comedies, first with her and Gerald's troupe and then later while touring the circuit. She acted in *What Happened to Jones* and from 1899 to 1900 she was at the Bijou in Jersey City, New Jersey, and the paper wrote, *"...a most meritorious performance of a difficult part is that of Ethel Hertslet, who appears as Alvira Starlight."* In 1901, Ethel performed in *Out of the Fold* in Utica, New York, at the Majestic Theatre. The *Utica Herald Dispatch* wrote on April 1, 1902, *"she was acceptable as Mrs. Cobb."* The four-act was based on the poem, *The Ninety and Nine*. It was called a stage picture of unusual dramatic power, scenery, and mechanical effects. In early 1903, she was Grandma Chazy Bunker in *Her Lord and Master,* and later that year she reprised her role as Mrs. Cobb in *Out of the Fold* until mid-1904. She then performed as Polly in *A Message from Mars,* where she appears, (although spelled Hertzlet) on the IBDB.com website for plays.

Ethel performed mostly in farce comedies, which according to Webster's 1892 *Common School Dictionary* were low comedies, being absurd, ludicrous, and unreal. They were written to entertain the audience with unlikely and extravagant, yet possible situations. They sometimes included mistaken identities, crude verbal humor including puns and sexual innuendo, and a fast-paced plot.

Opinions about the Victorian stage varied as is illustrated by a contrasting report in Birmingham, Alabama's *Age-Herald*, *"A farce actor or actress is a distinct type of player, gifted with the indiscernible element of merriment, which proves infections, contagious and untiring."* The generic "farce" label was applied to a whole host of performances in the 19th century, including minstrel, vaudeville, burlesque, and legitimate theater of the time. If the farce was performed in a single act farce then it was likely booked into vaudeville or burlesque theatres. However, if it included multiple acts, it likely played legitimate houses. Farce in its broadest sense was nearly as popular as melodrama, the stuff of touring acting companies living on the edge as they tramped from one town to the next.

Because theaters were not air-conditioned, plays and vaudeville shows generally ran from October through June. However, some troupes, including Ethel's seem to have stayed on the road longer. Plays were performed throughout the year in America, but Fall is when new shows were presented.

Ethel and her fellow actors, along with all their costumes and stage scenery toured doing one-nighters, split-weeks, or weekly stands, depending upon booking contracts, local population, and a theater's size.

Ethel Hartslet as Alvira Starlight

THE END OF ETHEL

Four generations of Hertslet women. Ethel is on the left with Jolette next to her. Seated is Auriol with her baby, Ann. Photo taken about 1937.

ETHEL'S LATER YEARS

To say that things went badly for Ethel and Gerald in California would be an understatement. Her change from the young, naïve Victorian socialite to a lonely ranch wife longing for a man to provide for her and love her, ended with abandonment and a sordid affair.

The Hertslet brothers had gained a reputation in the valley for not finishing their projects while Ethel doted on her ranch animals, cooked, cleaned, and became a mother three times over when Jolette, Victor, and Harold were born between 1886 and 1889. Her cousins Claude, Guy, and Ernest Barry arrived in 1887, and she finally had familial companionship. Ethel's mother-in-law sent them a maid named Gertrude Edith Forster to help with the daily duties once Ethel became pregnant with their first child. Edith married Ethel's cousin Claude in 1888, and they all lived nearby in Lake County.

Gerald's brothers left Burns Valley in 1887 and eventually returned to England. Ethel and Gerald stayed, and he was a local realtor with Thomas Beakbane. The youngest Hertslet son, Godfrey, explained why Gerald quit ranching and why his brothers Louis and Bernard left. *"The emigration to the United States had proved a dismal failure and a very costly experiment."* After failing at real estate, Gerald left for San Francisco to be an actor—something that Ethel longed to be again. With Gerald down in San Francisco, Ethel sought companionship with her cousins but grew especially close to the twenty-two-year-old, five-foot four, brown-eyed Claude. Gerald eventually sold the ranch at a loss and moved his family to San Francisco. Claude and Edith, as well as Guy and Ernest, followed. Ethel finally got her wish, and she and Gerald began touring the theater circuit, after taking their children back to England to be educated and cared for by their parents. Yet again, Gerald failed to make their acting stock company a success and was lured back to England for a premier acting gig, which also failed.

In the midst of all this, Ethel returned to the stage in San Francisco, but papers around the U.S. focused on her divorce. Many of them took great interest in the Hertslet divorce and sensationalized the doomed couple's plight. For whatever reason, the *London Times* never mentioned it. *The New York Times*, *Chicago Tribune*, and *San Francisco Chronicle* were just a few of the many who continued to follow their story. It took Gerald only one month to counter-sue his lovely wife for a divorce. In the midst of Ethel performing at Stockwell's on November 3, 1894, Gerald filed his divorce against her with some very prominent attorneys. They were Cormac & Donohue, counselors to the British Consulate in New York City, and Denis Donohue, who also had an office in San Francisco. His charges against her were a bit harsher, with him citing cruelty and her having been unduly intimate with other men, including all three of her cousins, Ernest, Guy, and especially Claude. Gerald claimed Ethel caused him great mental torture and much suffering, in addition to being cruel. The cruelty part was in reference to Ethel inducing him to go to London to accept the lucrative theatrical engagement that he failed miserably in. The newspaper reported that Gerald longed to return to San Francisco to settle the matter, but alas, he had no money for passage. One story reported their children Jolette, Victor, and Harold were living in England with Gerald's family because he claimed Ethel was unfit to be their mother. Another account claimed they were living with Ethel's parents, Charles and Edith Barry. It's likely eight-year-old Jolette was living with the Hertslets at Belle Vue House, while little Victor and Harold were with the Barry family at Gloucester Lodge.

Gerald later filed a cross-complaint citing Claude Barry as a co-respondent in the case. Claude, who was still dealing with his own divorce, was cited to appear before Judge Troutt in San Francisco on April 12, 1895, to "show cause" why he had not paid $20 ($536) a month alimony, $20 costs, and $50 ($1,340) counsel fees in the divorce proceedings of Claude Barry vs. Gertrude Barry, in accordance

THE END OF ETHEL · 103

with an order of the court. Showing up in court would have proved difficult for Claude since he was now living in New York City.

The Hertslets' torrid divorce dragged on, and on July 13, 1895, the *San Francisco Chronicle* ran a story in Ethel's favor. They reported Ethel wanted to be divorced from her cheating husband, and his absence was holding up the process. She also claimed his hold up was causing her theater career to suffer. A Minnesota paper, the *Winona Daily Republican* ran the same story, but its headline read, *DOMESTIC INFELICITY: MRS. HERTSLET MARRIED IN HASTE TO REPENT AT LEISURE.* On July 14, 1895, the Cleveland Plain Dealer covered the divorce with the same details but also added that Ethel wanted the divorce over with so she could take advantage of an offer from her parents to go home to England and live with them and her children. Their headline read, *HE MARRIED AGAINST THE WISHES OF HIS FATHER—HIS DOMESTIC TROUBLES.*

The Daily Tribune in Salt Lake City also reported details about the divorce, and the headline read, ACTRESS AND ARISTOCRAT. They rehashed many of the details from other newspapers, including the fact that Gerald's father was Sir Edward Hertslet, K.C.B. and Librarian of the foreign office of England. They also mentioned that Sir Edward did not want Gerald to marry Ethel, and they lost $100,000 ($2.68 million) on a farm in California.

As the divorce raged on like a western wild fire, more accusations appeared in the newspaper—even racier than before. This story's headline read, *HERTSLET'S STORY BY MAIL: HIS WIFE AND THE BROTHERS BARRY.* Even the reporter noted the latest testimony from Gerald was interesting, while other portions were simply revolting. It included statements from Gerald claiming he did nothing to wrong Ethel and never caused her any mental suffering. In fact, he claimed that she caused him great mental anguish with her intimacy with the Barry brothers, who are her first cousins. He charged Claude Barry with great intimacy with Ethel and said trouble arose over this on several occasions. Gerald stated that in 1891, while they were all living in Lake County, he caught Ethel kissing her cousin, Ernest. He stated he forbid Ernest from coming into their home until Ethel promised to never do it again. He couldn't exactly ban him since Ernest worked for Gerald. Later that year, Gerald was performing at Stockwell's in San Francisco while Ethel stayed back in Burns Valley. According to Gerald, she took the children across Lower Lake to live with Reverend Leigh Mann, and she was living alone with her other cousin, Guy Barry. Upon hearing this, Gerald immediately went back to Burns Valley and put an end to the supposed scandal.

Ethel stated Gerald's letters to her had been cold, and she was upset to learn from her cousin Guy that Gerald was in San Francisco spending all their money in saloons. As Guy was leaving this scene, he purposely kissed Ethel, and a fight broke out between him and Gerald. Gerald claims he forgave Ethel for her indiscretions. According to the deposition, they immediately sold the ranch at auction, and the family moved to San Francisco with Gerald. Their troubles did not stop even after the move, however, because Ethel's cousins moved there, as well. Another fight broke out over a supposed ring Guy gave to Ethel. The situation was patched up when Ethel gave the ring back to Guy with a note saying she could never see him again. However, Gerald claims Ethel violated this promise a year later in 1892 when she and her children met Guy for lunch across the San Francisco Bay at Mrs. Hartley's. To do this, she would have had to take the Sausalito Land and Ferry Company service because the Golden Gate Bridge would not be opened for another forty-five years.

The sordid deposition contained many charges of kissing, clandestine meetings, and much more. Among them was an incident that took place at the home where Ethel was staying at 302 Fourth Street, San Francisco in April 1894. Claude and Ernest had gone to the house to bid their farewells to Ethel. Guy was now married and did not enter the equation this time. Upon their departure, both cousins gave her a kiss. Gerald said, *"She told me then, that in March 1894, when she was sympathizing with him*

[Claude Barry] about some trouble he had with his wife that she had thrown her arms around his neck and kissed him." Gerald, of course, did not take kindly to her sympathetic gesture. He also mentioned that during the last two months of his time in San Francisco that Ethel and Claude were almost inseparable, and Claude often accompanied his wife to the Midwinter Fair, took frequent walks in the park, and often did not return until eleven at night. According to Gerald, when he questioned Ethel, she told him that they were simply cousins.

Ethel, of course, vehemently denied all of Gerald's accusations and said they were false and based on a flimsy foundation. She claims she bore the burden of their tragic life in Lake County where she cared for five horses, milked the cows, and conducted the ranch while her husband was away drinking and playing polo and tennis. She was living on an allowance of £100 (£8,440), which she claimed was being sent to England for the care of her children. She also declared she had no intention of marrying Claude Barry, who was living in New York City, or anyone else.

As if the Hertslet divorce wasn't spicy enough, the papers also tossed in Claude and Edith's. Their divorce was no less ugly, and Edith, who was no longer Ethel's domestic, was fighting her own issues. When Claude filed for divorce in October 1894, Edith was certain he had no intention of marrying his cousin Ethel. However, nine months later, Edith no longer believed that to be true and stated she would *"fight the divorce until the end."* When asked if she would comment on her friend, Mrs. Hertslet, she declined by saying, *"she had enough troubles of her own without receiving harsh words from her [Edith]."*

In the throes of their divorce, both Ethel and Gerald received tragic news. Around July 1895, Ethel received word from England that her first son, Victor, was gravely ill and immediately set sail for England. Not wanting the press to know any more details of her personal life, her attorney and the woman she lived with cited her reason for leaving as having to do with her divorce from Gerald. While that part may have been true, the papers never learned the real reason for her return to England. Her friend, Mrs. Captain Hartley of San Francisco stated, *"Mrs. Hertslet has not gone to England with a view of effecting reconciliation. She was compelled there because it was discovered that there was a fatal clause in the law, and she did not want to jeopardize her case, even if she did have to make the long journey. There were also medical reasons and a desire to keep her children from the possession of her husband. Mrs. Hertslet did not meet Claude Bery (sic) in New York. She will return to America."*

The *San Francisco Chronicle* made it seem like Ethel was enjoying her trip to England, but how were they to know? While Ethel may have been enjoying the company of her children and her parents, she must have been devastated and depressed to watch her eight-year-old son pass away on April 6, 1896, which was Easter Sunday. The paper reported that Victor Barry Hertslet tragically died at his grandfather's, Charles Ainslie Barry, at Sydenham-Hill in Kent after suffering a long illness. It's not known if Gerald was at his side with Ethel or not, but interestingly, the obituary in the *London Times* simply shows, "the son of Mrs. G. Hertslet." Clearly still in divorce mode, Gerald placed a separate obituary for Victor on April 14 in the Morning Post, which read, "the dearly loved-son of Gerald Spencer Hertslet." These two distinct obituaries show the hatred between the feuding couple. After the death of their son, Ethel and Gerald continued to lead separate lives—he in England and she in America.

Two years later, Gerald was granted a divorce by the New York Supreme Court in a special session on June 28, 1898, by Judge Nash. True to form, the cause for divorce contained some pretty nasty allegations, even by Victorian standards. Gerald filed the cause on June 22, 1898, and in it he stated from October 1897 until and including January 1898, Ethel and Claude resided together and committed acts of adulterous intercourse. He claimed they were committed without his consent, connivance, and privity. Since they were not previously divorced, nor had five years elapsed since their separation, she was accused of committing adultery. Upon being served with the papers, Ethel filed a complaint with her attorneys,

Swayne & Swayne. However, that complaint was withdrawn, and Ethel let the case go to court uncontested. A New York resident named Hal DeSilva, who resided at 215 Broadway, claimed he knew Ethel and Claude for over five years. During that time, he claimed Ethel told him there was an estrangement between her and her husband and that she had nothing to regret. She talked to him about living with her cousin Claude but never claimed they were married.

Since the sallow-complexioned Gerald's case prevailed, he was free to go on with his life as usual, but so was not the case for poor Ethel. The terms of the divorce were very specific. Gerald gained sole custody of their two remaining children, and Ethel was forbidden from marrying again until Gerald's death. The divorce decree contains these words, "that it shall be lawful for Gerald Spencer Hertslet, plaintiff, to marry again, in the same manner as if the said Ethel Marian Hertslet, the defendant, was actually dead; but it shall not be lawful for the defendant, Ethel Marian Hertslet to marry again until the said Gerald Spencer Hertslet shall be actually dead."

With Ethel finally free of Gerald, she began her acting career in earnest. Claude stayed put in Manhattan where he earned a living as an auditor and accountant as Ethel started her tour. Being an actress during the Victorian era was far from being an actress today, and stage morality was a common topic—with some arguing for and others against. Even though some considered the life of an actress to be less than acceptable early on, that stigma gradually reversed. By the turn of the century, Americans had changed the way they looked at actors.

Ethel was sharing the same stages, albeit not at the same time, with the likes of Maud Adams, Ethel Barrymore, and Lillie Langtry. Nicholas Temperley, curator of the University of Illinois Rare Book and Manuscript collection wrote, *"Women in this period enjoyed full acceptance, if not equality, as actors, and gradually lived down the moral ambiguity long attached to that profession. Theater in its many forms was evidently an entertainment for a broad range of social classes, excepting only those whose religion intervened."*

Ethel acted in the height of this movement and performed in various plays across the U.S., until 1905, while she lived with Claude in New York City. After her acting career ended, she stayed in the city with Claude but made frequent trips back to England. Until now, her two children were still living in England, but at the age of forty-two, she became a full-time mother again. Her seventeen-year-old son Harold decided to move to America, and on November 23, 1906, he boarded the S.S. *Minnetonka* in Southampton and left Grandmother Barry's home at Gloucester Lodge in Lewisham. He left his year-long job at the firm of T.H. Allan & Co., who owned the East India Coffee Merchants of Gracechurch Street in London. He was a clerk with them until he departed for America. On December 2, Ethel and Claude welcomed Harold at their New York City home, which was just a half block off Broadway at 542 W, 159th Street. Harold, who stood one inch above the 5'8" average for a Victorian gentleman, had a dark complexion with brown hair and brown eyes. He arrived just in time to celebrate Christmas with his mother. In early 1912, Harold married Helen Beardsley in New York City, and the year prior, Ethel's first child, Jolette, married Ronald Bruce Hay in London. In May 1913, Jolette and Bruce gave Ethel her first grandchild named Diana Auriol Hay, and Harold and Helen followed with Ethel's second grandchild named Victor in June of that same year.

The year 1916 arrived, and Harold joined the British military to serve in the war. He was at the Battle of the Somme, one of the costliest engagements of the First World War in terms of causalities. That summer the line of trenches on the Western Front stretched from the English Channel across the length of France to the Swiss border. The attack began with a predominately British force clambering out of its trenches and crossing "No Man's Land" under withering German machinegun and artillery fire. After the fury of their own barrage, they expected an easy walk onto the German lines. Instead, they were met by whizzing rifle fire, artillery, and rapid machine-guns that were seemingly unhurt by the bombardment. The attack ended in disaster for Great Britain, and they suffered almost sixty thousand casualties—making it the bloodiest day in British military history. Harold was one of them. When the news reached Ethel, she and Claude left their Broadway-area home and boarded the S.S. *St. Louis* in New York on July 2, 1916.

SOMEHOW, HAROLD KNEW

Harold's wife Helen and their son Victor visited him in England but returned to the safety of America on April 3, 1916, aboard the S.S. St. Paul. When they arrived in New York, she and Victor moved in with her father Edmund Beardsley in the Bronx. Whether they knew it or not, that was the last time they saw Harold. Three months later, Harold sat with hope and trepidation contemplating what would happen as he penned a tearful and gut-wrenching letter to Helen the night before the battle.

Harold Herslet, 1898

BEF, France, June 30, 1916

My own dearest Helen,
From here we are leaving for the trenches, and tomorrow morning the big attack of the war begins… In the last weeks my thoughts have been all with you, Vic, and in this hour of danger I am hoping only for your safety and happiness in case of my being killed. I am not afraid, but I only worry about not seeing you again in case of the worst. This is my only thought. I could go all right if it wasn't for that.
It is hard to write this letter as I am bad at telling you how I really feel. But I love you and Vic more than all the world, and the day we are reunited, if God wills it, will be the greatest day of my life.
I can't write more now, I must go and transfer my real thoughts to you through the air burning this night and tomorrow.
Goodbye darling if it is goodbye, look after Vic as I know you will.

Your very loving,
Harold

Two years later, in 1918, Gerald died. Now that he was actually dead, according to the terms of his divorce, she and Claude were free to become husband and wife after twenty years of living together. They wasted no time in mourning poor Gerald and were issued marriage license #16558 and married on June 11, 1918, in Manhattan.

Exactly two months after their marriage, a Norwegian ship named the *Bergensfjord* steamed into New York City's harbor. Eleven sailors and ten passengers onboard carried and suffered the effects of the

THE END OF ETHEL • 107

Spanish flu. It was the first of many ships arriving in New York with passengers and crew bringing the flu. It earned that name because most of the newspapers around the world were keeping the epidemic quiet, and Spain had the first paper to report the flu. Even though the War was coming to a close, it had created the perfect storm with poor health conditions, malnutrition, and wounded soldiers. The illness spread as soldiers crossed multiple countries to fight, transport goods, and go home. But this disease did not prey on the weak alone, and thousands of perfectly healthy men, women, and children succumbed to it. It came on suddenly with a fever, chills, headache, achy joints and bones, and acute bronchitis and often led to pneumonia. It killed people within forty-eight hours.

While Ethel and Claude were not affected by the flu, it did come close. Ethel's grandson Victor was struck down with it at the age of five. They were living in the city of five and one-half million people when he contracted it. Children like Victor were kept at home so he wouldn't spread the disease. Helen knew her son was very ill and running a high fever, so she called the doctor. After the doctor examined Victor, he advised there was really no medicine that worked. During this era doctors used a variety of remedies, many of which could be found in local drugstores. Patent medicines containing secret and trademarked ingredients were very popular including Vicks Vapo-Rub and atropine capsules (belladonna). Of course, these didn't treat the flu, but the medical practitioners of the day didn't know that or have anything else to help their patients. The doctor left saying he didn't expect Victor to make it through the night. Having more cases than he could no doubt handle, he left citing, "to see if he could help anyone else who had a better chance." When Ethel learned of this, she decided she was not going to let her only grandson die. She made him a mixture of whiskey, water, and sugar and stayed at his bedside all night. She gave him small amounts of this every fifteen to twenty minutes. When the doctor returned in the morning, he expected to find the young boy dead. Much to the doctor's surprise, Victor was still alive and starting to feel better. Ethel had saved her grandson's life the same way she had saved her Lake County kitten.

During the latter part of the 1920s, Claude and Ethel were transitioning their lives from New York City to England. Sometime in 1926, Ethel made a trip to England, and in late June 1927, Claude left for England. The sixty-five-year-old accountant departed on the S.S. *Minnekahda* and arrived in Liverpool on July 5. He made his way to their new home called Barrymore on Fern Road in Storrington, Sussex, and must have been getting things settled before he brought Ethel over with him. He returned to Ethel and his American home at 327 W. 56th Street in New York City aboard the S.S. *Baltic* on October 10, 1927.

After living in America for over forty years, Ethel finally realized her dream of returning to her birth country. While living in Storrington, Ethel gained a bit of a quirky reputation. As she began to age, she began showing signs of senility. According to a family story that is still told today, Ethel was known as the "Mad Witch of Storrington." While no official records survive or indicate this was true, it's something her family members have passed down through the generations. They also advised the nickname was a form of endearment regarding a highly eccentric, unusual old woman. It seems she gained this moniker for the "nutty" or witch-like things she did. For one, she would open the window of her home and place a wooden plank on it so the animals could come in out of the cold at night. Another quirk involved carrying a portable heater to St. Mary's church with her so she and the animals that followed her would stay warm along their way. It seems her love of animals had crossed the pond with her.

Jolette's descendants recall Ethel as "Granny Barry" and shared a story about her shopping at Selfridge's in London. Selfridge's store in the late 1920s was a marvel and *Architectural Design Magazine* called the newly completed Oxford Street flagship "the most imperial building in London." In the 1930s, the store's Silver Jubilee earned Gordon Selfridge accolades. *"He has not merely transformed Oxford Street into one of the world's finest shopping centres,"* wrote *Drapers Record*, *"he gave a lead to the entire store trade."* As Ethel sat in this marvel, she had "minions" run all over Selfridge's and other London stores for her needs.. They went to Harrods and other stores to do her shopping so she wouldn't have to traipse all over. They would bring everything to her for approval, and she'd either keep it or send it back.

Claude and Ethel remained together until September 25, 1936, when her cousin, companion, partner, and husband for more than sixty years, passed away. Claude was seventy-four-years-old when he died and was living at Barrymore. Claude was buried in St. Mary's church cemetery in Storrington with a headstone simply marked with his name, birth and death dates, and R I P.

Shortly after Claude's death, Ethel traveled back to New York. On February 19, 1937, the seventy-two-year-old, white-haired Ethel boarded the S.S. *President Harding* for New York. She indicated she would be living with daughter-in-law, Mrs. Helen Hertslet, at 9213 95th Street, Woodhaven, Queens. The ship's manifest indicated Ethel carried a medical certificate identifying her as senile. No records could be found to determine how long Ethel stayed in New York, but she eventually made her way back home to England. By March 1937, Ethel was no longer listed in the Storrington phone book or anywhere else for that matter.

Ethel's quest for happiness may have been her motive for moving to the southern English community of Rye sometime between 1937 and 1938. She had no known family or ties to the area, and it's about two hours due East of Storrington. The town is located in the East Sussex countryside in the southeast of England. It sits on a hill overlooking the River Rother and Romney Marsh. While there, Ethel lived at West Watch Studio in Traders Passage.

Remember the wealthy nobleman Ethel reportedly ditched to marry Gerald? Well, he may have reemerged in Ethel's life at this time. No data could be found to determine the true identity of the nobleman, but it's entirely possible he was an Irishman named Charles Evelyn Cramer-Roberts, and there are many reasons for this possibility.

First, Charles came from a well-to-do Irish family in County Kildare who was in her social class. The Cramer-Roberts were land barons, sheriffs, and magistrates in the county but did not carry titles. Charles's mother was the daughter of a wealthy Dubliner as well. When Charles Evelyn was born in Sallymount, Kildare, on March 21, 1866, his father was employed as the high sheriff. Between 1879 and 1882, Charles attended Christ's College, End Village, Finchley, England (CCF) at the age of fourteen with his older brother Cecil J.R. Cramer-Roberts.

This is the area where Ethel lived out her last couple of years with Charles Cramer-Roberts.

He was back in England by April 1891 as a twenty-five-year-old boarder living on his own means, slightly west of London, in New Windsor, Berkshire. He arrived in America in September 1891 and on June 9, 1900, was living at 365 Henry Street in Brooklyn as a boarder and was employed as a clerk. It's interesting to note that both Charles and Ethel were living very near to each other in New York City. One has to wonder if they each knew the other was living there. It appears Charles stayed in New York for about five years because on December 16, 1911, Charles was still in Brooklyn, New York. He planned a dinner at the Waldorf Hotel for the "Old Boys" of the school who were living in the city. A few years later, one of the Old Boys writing from Newark, New Jersey, said he often came across Charles.

Nearly two years after Ethel left New York, Charles followed. He departed America for good on June 12, 1932, and traveled to his new home in Drumbanager, County Armagh, Northern Ireland. He was a sixty-six-year-old salesman traveling in third-class aboard the S.S. California. By November 1938, Charles had moved back to England and was residing at the Mermaid Hotel in Rye, East Sussex, in the same town where Ethel was residing.

WHO WAS CHARLES CRAMER-ROBERTS?

Charles' mother, Elizabeth "Lizzie," was the daughter of a wealthy Dubliner, while his father, Charles Torin Cramer-Roberts, hailed from Sallymount, Kildare County. Charles Torin served as high sheriff of Newbridge, Kildare County, before moving the family to Paddington, England, by 1871. They later returned to Ireland, but tragedy struck in 1877 when eleven-year-old Charles Evelyn lost his father, who was only forty.

Charles and his brother Cecil moved back to England, where Charles attended Christ's College, Finchley, from 1879 to 1882. Entering the school at age twelve, he studied a wide range of subjects, including English, Geography, Classics, Mathematics, and languages like French and German. Athletics were an integral part of school life, and Charles was notably active in cricket, track events, and other competitions. In 1882, he participated in several events such as the 100-yard dash, the quarter-mile race, hurdles, and the three-legged race. Although younger than many competitors, he held his own in these physically demanding sports. He also enjoyed Fives, a fast-paced handball-like game, reaching the final of the Under-16 Singles in 1881–82. However, he did not participate in rugby, swimming, or the school play.

After leaving school before his sixteenth birthday, Charles returned to Dublin to live with his mother and grandfather at 23 Fitzwilliam Place. He became an early member of the Old Finchleians, an alumni group formed in 1876. By 1891, at age twenty-five, he was living independently in New Windsor, Berkshire, before emigrating to America, where he worked as a clerk and rented a room in Brooklyn. He frequently traveled back to Dublin to visit his mother and brother, maintaining close ties to his family.

Standing 5'7", Charles lived a transatlantic life, shuttling between New York, Dublin, and England until the early 1930s. Despite his many moves, he remained connected to his roots and the friends and traditions of his youth.

It would take fifty-three years until Ethel and her nobleman were reunited, and at the age of seventy-four, Ethel met Charles in Rye, and they were married. On November 3, 1938, she wed Charles Evelyn Cramer-Roberts at St. Anthony's Catholic Church in Rye, despite them both being Protestant. Their witnesses were Marty Gordon and Bridget McKenna. It's not known if they knew these people or they were simply witnesses, but Bridget also lived at the Mermaid Hotel.

After being married, they resided at Ethel's Rye home at West Watch Studio in Traders Passage. About two weeks after their marriage, on November 22, 1938, Ethel changed her will. She appointed Lloyds

Bank London as her executor and trustee. She advised they would act as her banker and perform any service on behalf of her estate. She also appointed Dawes, Son, and Prentice of Bank Chamber, Rye as her attorney for the estate and gave them power of attorney as they saw fit for her estate. Her will advised that she wished the bank to sell all her property and personal estate and turn it into cash. She noted that any sale was held at the discretion of her appointees and that the money should be used to pay for her funeral and testamentary expenses, as well any outstanding debts. The rest of the money was to be invested as the bank saw fit for the residuary trust moneys. Her will also advised that her trust, "pay the income thereof my husband the said Charles Evelyn Cramer-Roberts during his life and from after his death. In trust as to both capital and income of the Residuary Trust Fund for my grandson Victor Beardsley Hertslet and my granddaughter Diana Auriol Haward of 9 Chester Place Hyde Park, London, in equal shares absolutely."

At age seventy-four, Ethel endured many highs and lows in her life. She lost both of her sons, dealt with an estranged daughter, was blessed with two grandchildren, one great-grandchild that she knew about, divorced one husband, lost another, and was seemingly enjoying life with her third. While living out her senior years with husband number three, she boarded a bus bound for the seaside town of Jesson, which was renamed St. Mary's Bay in 1935, some fifteen miles from Rye on December 8, 1938. After she finished her business, she was ready to head back to Rye, so she went to the bus stop, which was near the post office. About 4:45 p.m., a woman named Ethel Florence "St. Florence" Best was waiting at the corner to catch her bus to Hythe. That's when she noticed Ethel crossing the street from the seaside section of the road. She approached "St. Florence" and asked her if she knew what time the Rye bus arrived. Others standing nearby told her they thought it was in the next few minutes, which is why they thought it odd when Ethel stepped back into the street and headed toward the ocean. Both the corner and the street were dark, so Ethel didn't see twenty-nine-year-old Sidney Luckhurst coming. Despite his bicycle having a light, the two collided. She was knocked to the ground, and he was thrown from his bike. Standers-by rushed to assist them. Ethel was taken into the post office where officer P.C. Shibley arrived to take statements.

Ethel stated, *"It was not his fault, but I don't know what happened."* Luckhurst told Shipley he was riding toward the town of Dymchurch when Ethel suddenly darted out in from of him. He swerved to miss her, but his pedal caught her in the leg. She was taken to the Royal Victoria Hospital in nearby Folkestone where she was treated for severe shock, a fractured and cut right leg, and a cut and swelling over her left eye. Despite the incident, she was doing well until December 15, when she suddenly became worse. At about 3 p.m. on December 16, 1938, Ethel passed away from pneumonia. It was common with elderly people who remained in the same position for long periods and fluids settled in one area of the lungs, which increased the susceptibility of infection. Her death was ruled accidental.

The newspaper story headline read, *RYE WOMAN'S FATAL ACCIDENT. THREE WEEKS AFTER MARRIAGE.* Even though there is mention of her being newly married, the story never mentioned Charles. It did state that her son-in-law, Colonel Ronald Bruce Hay, provided evidence of her marriage and that in fact it was only three weeks. It is curious that Charles did not appear in this story and Bruce identified her.

Ethel is buried in Hawkinge Cemetery, which is just outside Folkestone in grave number T 840. She lies in her unmarked grave with no headstone, alone, and with no family around her. County officials do not know if she ever had a headstone, but her estate was not settled until March 1939. At some point, Charles went back to his home country and resided in Dublin in early 1939. He died fifty-four days after Ethel in Hume Street Hospital Dublin on February 9 of heart failure. Charles is buried with his mother Elizabeth Hamilton Cramer-Roberts, his grandparents James Alexander and Rosetta Hamilton, and his great-grandfather, General Robert Gorges Hamilton in Mt. Jerome, Dublin, Ireland.

INDEX

Beef
    Chili con Carne, 76
    Roast Beef with Gravy, 75
    Steak and Onions, fried, 75

Beverages
    Gin Fizz, 36
    Ice Cream Soda, 11
    Russian Cocktail, 35
    Tea, 34

Bread
    Currant Loaf, 18
    Rock Cakes, 17
    Sourdough, 20
    White, 14

Breakfast
    Porridge, 9
    Strawberries and Whipped Cream, 12

Cakes
    Simnel, 88
    Sponge, 85
    Tipsy, 84
    Victoria Sandwiches, 87

Candy
    English Toffee, Grandma Nita's, 97
    Fudge, Grandma Nita's Marshmallow, 96

Condiments
    Tomato Ketchup, 44

Desserts
    Compote of Pears, 83
    Ice Cream, vanilla, 99
    Meringues, 94
    Mincemeat, 93

Dressing
    Bacon Lemon, 70

Eggs
    Curried, 22
    Scrambled, 21

Fish
    Salmon Cakes, 67
    Salmon Cutlets with Caper Sauce, 66
    Trout, pan-roasted, 64
    Trout, Whole Fried, 63

Jellies & Jams
    Apple Jelly, 23
    Apricot Jam, 26
    Peach Jam, 27
    Port Wine Jelly, 24

Lamb
    Mutton Cutlets, 79
    Mutton Stew, 78

Pies & Pastries
    Apple Jelly Tarts, 30
    Apple Tart, 31
    Blackberry Tart, 32
    Cheesecake Tarts, 29
    Crust, 94
    Marmalade Tartlets, 29
    Mince, 93
    Peach Tart, 32

Pork
    Loin, 71
    Toad in the Hole, 72

Poultry
    Chicken, roast, 68
    Turkey, roast, 70

Pudding
    Bread and Butter, 89
    Corn Starch, 91
    Custard, 92
    Plum, 90

Salads
    Cabbage, with Dressing, 41
    Lettuce and Tomato w/ French Dressing, 60

Sauces
    Tomato, 59

Seafood
    Crab, dressed, 80
    Oysters, pickled, 81

Side Dishes
    Applesauce, 52
    Figs, pickled, Mrs. Beakbane's, 42
    Macaroni Neapolitaine, 59
    Mashed Potatoes, 50
    Potatoes, Browned, 51
    Sage & Onion Stuffing, 49

Soup
  Pea, 39
  Vegetable, 40
Vegetables
  Asparagus, 47
  Beans, French, 53
  Beets, boiled, 52
  Carrots, glazed, 54
  Cucumbers, Dressed, 55
  Lima Beans, 57
  Parsnips, boiled, 49
  Peas, boiled, 48
  Potatoes, Sweet, baked, 51
  Squash, Summer, 56
  Tomatoes, baked, 56
  Turnips, mashed, 59

RECIPE CREDITS

Apple Jelly Tarts: Recipe adapted from *Mrs. Beeton's Dictionary of Every Day of Cookery,* London, 1865.

Apple Jelly: Recipe adapted from *The Daily Examiner* (San Francisco), March 23, 1884.

Apple Tart: Recipe adapted from the *Cheyenne Daily Ledger,* April 26, 1876.

Apricot Jam: Recipe adapted from *Mrs. Beeton's Dictionary of Every Day of Cookery,* London, 1865.

Asparagus: Recipe adapted from *Mrs. Beeton's Dictionary of Every Day of Cookery,* London, 1865.

Baked Tomatoes: Recipe adapted from *Mrs. Beeton's Dictionary of Every Day of Cookery,* London, 1865.

Beans, French: Recipe adapted from *The Englishwoman's Cookery Book* by Isabella Mary Beeton, 1874.

Beets, boiled: Recipe adapted from *The Englishwoman's Cookery Book* by Isabella Mary Beeton, 1874.

Blackberry tart: Recipe adapted from *The Englishwoman's Cookery Book* by Isabella Mary Beeton, London, 1874.

Bread & butter pudding: Recipes adapted from *The Englishwoman's Cookery Book* by Isabella Mary Beeton, London, 1874.

Cabbage: with dressing: Recipe by author based on Ethel's description.

Carrots: Recipe adapted from, *Lessons in Cookery, Handbook of the National training school for cookery* (South Kensington, London), National Training School for Cookery (Great Britain), 1878.

Cheesecake Tarts: Recipe from the Perris Progress (California), October 26, 1916.

Chicken, roast: Recipe adapted from *Mrs. Beeton's Dictionary of Every Day of Cookery,* London, 1865.

Chili con Carne: Recipe adapted from *The Times,* Los Angeles, California, October 16, 1898.

Compote of pears: Recipe adapted from *Mrs. Beeton's Dictionary of Every Day of Cookery,* London, 1865.

Corn Starch pudding: adapted from, *Lessons in Cookery, Hand-book of the National training school for Cookery* (South Kensington, London), National Training School for Cookery (Great Britain), 1878.

Crab, dressed: Recipe adapted from *The Englishwoman's Cookery Book,* London, 1900s

Cucumbers: Recipe adapted from *Mrs. Beeton's Dictionary of Every Day of Cookery*, London, 1865.

Currant Loaf: recipe adapted from *International Gazette* (Buffalo, NY), May 3, 1902.

Curried Eggs: Recipe adapted from *The Uttoxeter New Era* (England), July 18, 1888.

Custard Pudding: Recipe adapted from *The Englishwoman's Cookery Book* by Isabella Mary Beeton, 1874.

English Toffee: Grandma Nita's, Recipe from Patricia Sparacino.

Figs, pickled: Mrs. Manzanita Beakbane's, from her granddaughter.

Fudge, Grandma Nita's Marshmallow: Recipe from Patricia Sparacino.

Gin Fizz: Recipe from *The Bar-Tender's Guide; or How to Mix All Kinds of Plain and Fancy Drinks,* Jerry Thomas, New York, 1887.

Ice cream soda: *Saxe's New Guide, or, Hints to Soda Water Dispensers,* 1894.

Ice cream: Recipe adapted from *Mrs. Beeton's Cookery Book,* London, 1900.

Lettuce and Tomato with French dressing: *The Manchester Courier,* August 16, 1905.

Lima Beans: Recipe adapted from *Brooklyn, NY, The Standard Union,* March 18, 1893.

Macaroni Neapolitaine: Recipe adapted from *The World, Evening Edition,* New York City, May 29, 1893.

Marmalade tartlets: Recipe adapted from *Mrs. Beeton's Dictionary of Every Day of Cookery,* London, 1865.

Meringues: Recipe adapted from *Mrs. Beeton's Dictionary of Every Day of Cookery,* London, 1865.

Mince Pie: Recipe adapted from *Mrs. Beeton's Dictionary of Every Day of Cookery,* London, 1865.

Mutton Cutlets: Recipe adapted from the *Lessons in Cookery, Hand-book of the National Training School for Cookery* (South Kensington, London), 1878.

Mutton Stew: Recipe adapted from *Mrs. Beeton's Cookery Book,* London, 1900.

Oysters, pickled: Recipe adapted from *The Brooklyn Daily Eagle,* January 20, 1906

Parsnips: *The Englishwoman's Cookery Book* by Isabella Mary Beeton, 1874.

Pea Soup: Recipe adapted from the *Lessons in Cookery, Hand-book of the National Training School for Cookery* (South Kensington, London), 1878.

Peach Jam: Recipe adapted from *The Daily Examiner* (San Francisco), September 28, 1918.

Peach Tart: Recipe adapted from *The Englishwoman's Cookery Book* by Isabella Mary Beeton, London, 1874.

Peas: *The Englishwoman's Cookery Book* by Isabella Mary Beeton, 1874.

Pie Crust: Recipe was created by the author based on typical 1800s recipes.

Plum Pudding: Recipe adapted from, *Lessons in Cookery, Hand-book of the National training school for Cookery* (South Kensington, London), National Training School for Cookery (Great Britain), 1878.

Pork Loin with Applesauce: Recipes adapted from the *Englishwoman's Cookery Book* by Isabella Mary Beeton, London, 1874.

Porridge: Recipe adapted from *The Manchester Weekly Times* (England), May 29, 1886.

Port Wine Jelly: Recipe adapted from *The Daily Examiner* (San Francisco), June 2, 1880.

Potatoes, browned: Recipe adapted from, *Lessons in Cookery, Hand-book of the National training school for Cookery* (South Kensington, London), National Training School for Cookery (Great Britain), 1878.

Potatoes, mashed: Recipe adapted from *Mrs. Beeton's Dictionary of Every Day of Cookery,* London, 1865.

Potatoes, Sweet, mashed: London's *The Daily Telegraph,* December 25, 1905.

Roast Beef with Gravy: Recipe adapted from *The Englishwoman's Cookery Book* by Isabella Mary Beeton, London, 1874.

Rock Cakes: *Lessons in Cookery, Hand-book of the National training school for Cookery* (South Kensington, London), National Training School for Cookery (Great Britain), 1879.

Russian Cocktail: Recipes from *The Daily Examiner,* July 15, 1888 & *The World's Drinks and How to Mix* Them by William "Cocktail" Boothby, 1907.

Sage and Onion Dressing: *The Englishwoman's Cookery Book* by Isabella Mary Beeton, 1874.

Salmon Cakes: Recipe adapted from the Englishwoman's Cookery Book by Isabella Mary Beeton, London, 1874.

Salmon Cutlets with Caper Sauce: Recipe adapted from *Mrs. Beeton's Dictionary of Every Day of Cookery,* London, 1865.

Scrambled Eggs: *Lessons in Cookery, Hand-book of the National training school for Cookery* (South Kensington, London), National Training School for Cookery (Great Britain), 1879.

Simnel Cake: This Buszard's cake recipe appeared in a 1909 *Los Angeles Times* story.

Sourdough Bread: *The Daily Examiner,* February 5, 1882.

Sponge Cake: *Mrs. Beeton's Cookery Book,* London, 1900.

Steak & Onions, Fried: *Recipe adapted from the Lessons in Cookery, Hand-book of the National training school for Cookery* (South Kensington, London), National Training School for Cookery (Great Britain), 1879.

Strawberries & Whipped Cream: *San Francisco's, The Daily Examiner,* July 16, 1887.

Summer Squash: Recipe adapted from *San Francisco's The Daily Examiner,* September 19, 1886.

Tea: Recipe adapted from *The Hampshire Advertiser* (England), September 21, 1889.

Tipsy Cake: Recipe adapted from *Mrs. Beeton's Dictionary of Every Day of Cookery,* London, 1865.

Toad in the Hole: adapted from, *Lessons in Cookery, Hand-book of the National training school for Cookery* (South Kensington, London), National Training School for Cookery (Great Britain), 1878.

Tomato Ketchup: adapted from the *California Recipe Book,* Sacramento, CA, 1872.

Trout, pan-fried: Recipe adapted from the *Kansas City Journal,* May 7, 1899.

Trout, whole fried: Recipe adapted from *The Weekly Bee* (Sacramento), June 24, 1882

Turkey, roast: Recipes adapted from the *Englishwoman's Cookery Book* by Isabella Mary Beeton, London, 1874.

Turnips, mashed: *The Englishwoman's Cookery Book* by Isabella Mary Beeton, 1874.

Vegetable Soup: Recipe adapted from *Mrs. Beeton's Dictionary of Every Day of Cookery,* London, 1865.

Victoria sandwiches: Recipe adapted from The Englishwoman's Cookery Book, London, 1900s

White Bread: Recipe adapted from Marion Harland's Breakfast, Luncheon and Tea, 1875.

ACKNOWLEDGMENTS

A world of thanks to Ethel's descendants Feather, Elizabeth, and Nicola, for sharing their stories, correspondence, and photos. Also, to Pat Sparacino who is a descendant of the Beakbanes. Thanks to my friend and author Chris Enss for bringing this book idea to Roan & Weatherford and to Casey Cowan for believing in it and publishing it.

ABOUT THE AUTHOR

Sherry Monahan began her writing career when she combined her passion for food, travel, and history. She penned her first book, *Taste of Tombstone,* in 1998. That same passion landed her a monthly magazine column in 2009 when she began writing her food column in *True West* entitled *Frontier Fare.*

Sherry is a culinary historian who enjoys researching the genealogy of food and spirits. While there's still plenty to explore about frontier food, she's expanding her culinary repertoire to include places and foods from all over America and beyond. She holds memberships in the James Beard Foundation, the Author's Guild, and the Wild West History Association.